Step-by-Step Tutorials

WEDGE QUILT WORKSHOP

10 Stunning Projects

Christina Cameli

stash BOOKS.

an imprint of C&T Publishing

Text copyright © 2017 by Christina Cameli

Photography and artwork copyright © 2017 by C&T Publishing, Inc.

PUBLISHER: Amy Marson

CREATIVE DIRECTOR: Gailen Runge

EDITORS: Karla Menaugh and Liz Aneloski

TECHNICAL EDITOR: Debbie Rodgers

COVER/BOOK DESIGNER: April Mostek

PRODUCTION COORDINATOR: Tim Manibusan

PRODUCTION EDITOR: Jennifer Warren

ILLUSTRATOR: Kirstie L. Pettersen

PHOTO ASSISTANT: Mai Yong Vang

HAND MODEL: Kristi Visser

STYLE PHOTOGRAPHY by Lucy Glover and
INSTRUCTIONAL PHOTOGRAPHY by Diane Pedersen of C&T Publishing, Inc.,
unless otherwise noted

Published by Stash Books, an imprint of C&T Publishing, Inc., P.O. Box 1456, Lafayette, CA 94549

Library of Congress Cataloging-in-Publication Data

Names: Cameli, Christina, 1976- author.

Title: Wedge quilt workshop : step-by-step tutorials--10 stunning projects / Christina Cameli.

Description: Lafayette, CA : Stash Books, an imprint of C&T Publishing, Inc., [2017]

Identifiers: LCCN 2017021741 | ISBN 9781617454981 (soft cover)

Subjects: LCSH: Patchwork quilts. | Patchwork--Patterns. | Quilting--Patterns. | Machine quilting--Patterns.

Classification: LCC TT835 .C356174 2017 | DDC 746.46--dc23

LC record available at https://lccn.loc.gov/2017021741

Printed in China

10 9 8 7 6 5 4 3 2 1

Dedication

To my father, Michael Cameli—a role model of strength, patience, kindness, and love

Acknowledgments

Wedge Quilt Workshop exists because of the incredible support I received during its creation. This book was a bigger project than I'd done before, and the writing of it coincided with the process of my divorce. I found myself needing help in a way I never had, and was humbled by the immense care and willing assistance that flowed from my community in response.

To C&T Publishing, thank you for graciously adapting the book schedule to my challenges and delays. And to my editor, Karla Menaugh, thank you for handling more anxiety and tearful conversations than any book editor should have to, for guiding me when I needed direction, and for resolving every concern I unearthed.

To Michael Miller Fabrics, thank you for the quick and bountiful supply of Cotton Couture that makes up all the solids for the quilts in this book. Thank you again and again for your help when it was most needed.

To Zihna Weiss, thank you for your joyful presence with my children as I worked, and for your continuous bright spirit and invaluable flexibility.

To my sister, Kaila Cameli, thank you for the afternoons, the evenings, the weekends, the movies, the sushi, the encouragement, and the playful generosity you bring to our home.

To my friend Shannon McNair, thank you for the heaps of encouragement and for believing this work has worth that is measured in something other than dollars.

To my most generous friends and colleagues, thank you for taking my work into your lap and finishing the binding: Juline Bajada, Michelle Freedman, Laura Gurley, Elsa Hart, Sam Hunter, Anna Long, and Elise Makler. You truly saved the day.

To Nancy Stovall, thank you for taking on an especially big project with an absurdly tight deadline. There is no way the book could have been completed without your quilting, or for that matter, without your laughter and hugs at every drop-off and pickup. I am indebted to you for the great gifts of your artistic vision and brilliant spirit.

To Bill Volckening, thank you for the generous use of quilts from the Volckening Collection. I am so grateful for the work you do, not only as your friend and colleague but also as a human and quilter at large.

And to all my readers, students, and online connections—know that every kind word, every enthusiastic comment, and every "just checking in" email kept me going and believing that this work was worth it. You kept me believing that I am a part of something special that is so much bigger than any of us individually.

You are all in this book. May you delight in it as cocreators. Without you, there would be only a dream unfinished; with you, magic appeared.

CONTENTS

Projects

BASIC ROUND CONSTRUCTION 18

ROUND VARIATIONS 38

BEYOND ROUNDS 66

WHY WEDGES?

A few years ago, I made an impulse purchase of a wedge ruler at my local quilt shop. I was drawn in by the idea of making a large one-patch circle without needing to draft my own pattern piece. I played around with different designs and slowly fell more and more in love with this wonderful shape.

And I'm not alone! Quilters have been playing with wedges for a long time, as these quilts from the Volckening Collection show.

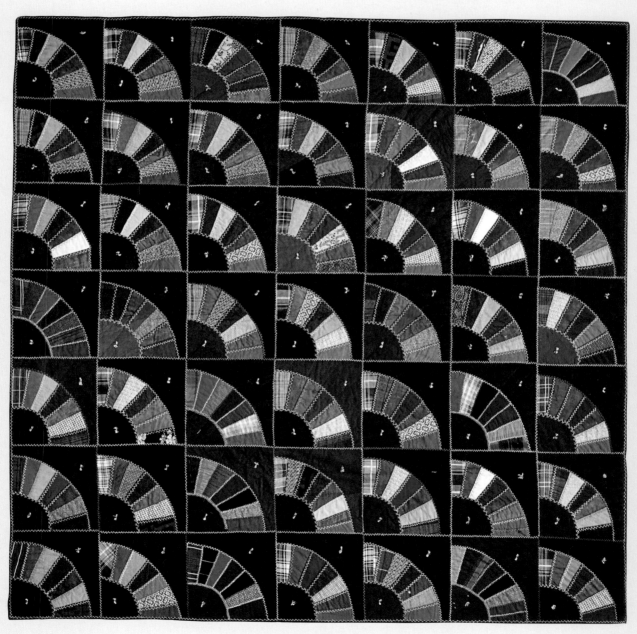

Image courtesy of the Volckening Collection

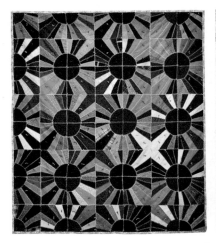

Images courtesy of the Volckening Collection

A beloved quilt made by my great-grandmother features a Dresden Plate design. Some of the wedges have worn away, but the fabric beneath still holds. I keep this quilt on my bed. It is my connection to a woman I never met—a woman whose life in some ways shaped mine. Whenever I sew my wedge creations to their backgrounds or finish their centers, I smile, realizing that generations before she had done the very same.

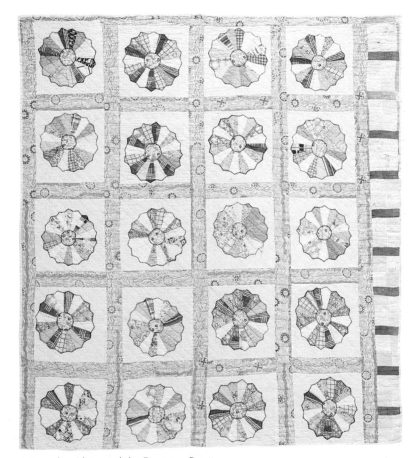

A Dresden Plate quilt by Beatrice Dority

I went down a few dead ends with my impulse purchase. But through optimism, experimentation, and error, I refined an approach to making rounds that came together reliably. I found that I loved working with wedges because it was a quick path to a bold quilt design. By cutting a group of basic wedges and putting them together, I was able to create a stunning product without much technical skill. That is attractive to me as a quilter because I tend to value design and impact more than technical proficiency.

You can imagine my delight, then, when I discovered wide vistas of design potential as I started doing more than making simple rounds. I was thrilled to find that when I cut up my wedge creations and sewed them together, my points matched up. If even *I* could get good results with wedges, other quilters needed to know about it!

So here I am, telling you there is a world of fun to be had with these shapes. Wedges are versatile and captivating. They make dynamic, graphic designs possible without complicated math or drafting. They make precision attainable without foundation paper piecing. Above all, wedges make it simple to jump in to a whole new type of quilt that, to my eyes, has limitless potential for the modern quilter.

If you like new challenges and discoveries, I imagine that this versatile approach to patchwork will delight you as it did me. Take some time to read my tips for making your wedge journey a success, and then see where it takes you!

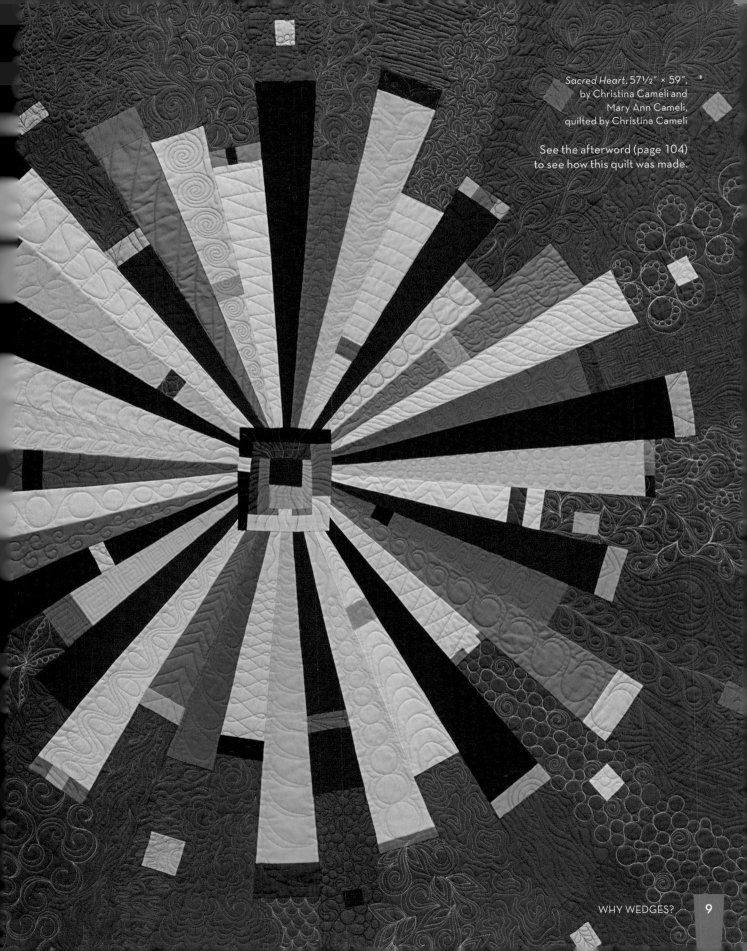

Sacred Heart, 57½″ × 59″,
by Christina Cameli and
Mary Ann Cameli,
quilted by Christina Cameli

See the afterword (page 104)
to see how this quilt was made.

WEDGE BASICS

A wedge is a portion of a circle. Put the right number of wedges together, and you'll have a complete circle. Wedges come in many sizes, though I've limited the ones in this book to just a couple. What all wedges have in common is that they have a wide end and a narrow end.

A wedge is measured by the angle formed where the two slanted sides meet. This angle is measured by degrees. If you're working with a template or a wedge ruler, you don't have to worry about the angle at all—the ruler or template designer has already done the work for you. You just need to know how many wedges you need to make a complete 360° circle.

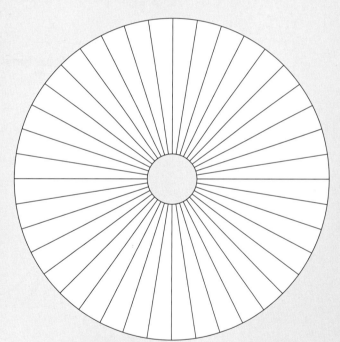

To make a whole round, use 40 of the 9° wedges.

For 9° wedges, use 40 wedges to make a circle (360° ÷ 9° = 40).

For 10° wedges, use 36 wedges to make a circle (360° ÷ 10° = 36).

For 15° wedges, use 24 wedges to make a circle (360° ÷ 15° = 24).

Wedge Rulers

This book includes a wedge pattern for every project, but if you have room in your budget for an acrylic wedge ruler, I'd recommend getting one or two. Wedge rulers make it easier to cut wedge shapes. They come in many shapes and sizes, and there are even extenders to make extra-large circles.

The width of a cut wedge at its widest point determines how wide the resulting circle will be. Some wedge rulers have markings that show the distance from the center of the finished circle to the edge of the wedge. Check the packaging of your wedge ruler to understand its markings.

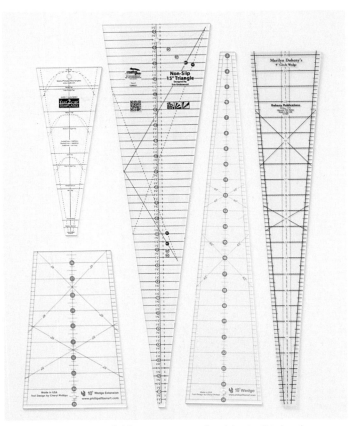

Wedge rulers are available in a variety of widths. In this book, the projects are made with 9° and 10° rulers.

Many wedge rulers do not produce a complete circle. Instead, they produce a circle with a hole in the center to avoid the buildup that happens when dozens of seams all come together at the center point. The width of the cut wedge at its narrowest point determines how wide the open inner circle will be. See Finishing the Curved Edges (page 25) to learn several techniques for finishing the open center.

Wedge Possibilities

With just one wedge ruler, you have many possibilities. The illustration at the right shows how different sizes of wedges can be cut from the same-width fabric strip.

If the large and small wedges at the right were each used to create a full round, the resulting rounds would be very different. The larger wedge makes a round that is larger in scale than that of the small wedge, and the hole in the center is bigger.

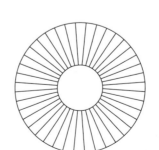

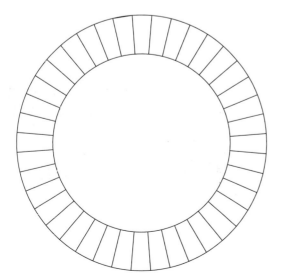

Cutting Wedge Shapes

An excellent technique for cutting wedges from scraps is cutting wedge shapes individually. When cutting from yardage, however, wedges are generally cut from strips of fabric.

Wedge shapes can be cut from strips in three ways:

- **In-line cutting** allows you to cut identical wedges from pieced, directional, or gradient fabric. The wide end is cut from the same side of the fabric for each wedge. Fabric between the wedges is wasted—although you may be able to use the scraps between to cut smaller wedges for other rounds. *Fig. A*

- **Reciprocal cutting** rotates the ruler between each cut. This produces more wedges from the same amount of fabric because there is no wasted fabric between cut wedges. If you are cutting from a solid fabric strip, you will have identical wedges. If you are cutting from a pieced strip or a fabric with stripes or other directional patterns, the wedges cut with the wide end up will be different from the wedges cut with the wide end down. See the instructions in Reciprocal Cutting (page 14). *Figs. B & C*

- **Angled cutting** produces identical slanted or pointed pieced wedges. To make an angled cut, first choose a guiding line (these are printed on many wedge rulers). You can create a guiding line with a piece of masking tape, if needed.

Align the guiding line with either the edge of the fabric or a seam on the pieced fabric. The fabric between the wedges will be wasted.

If you use pieced strip sets, as in the example, stagger the strips as you sew the strip set together, loosely following the angle of the wedge that you are going to cut. This will waste less fabric (see Slanted Wedges, page 42). *Figs. D & E*

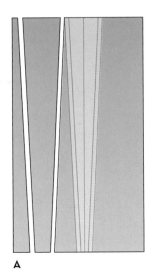

A

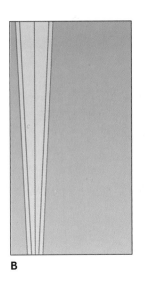

B

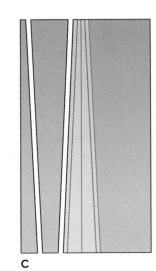

C

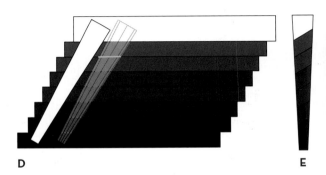

D

E

RECIPROCAL CUTTING

Most patterns in this book use reciprocal cutting.

❶ Align the fabric strip with a horizontal line on the cutting mat. Find the centerline of the wedge ruler, and align that centerline with a vertical line on the cutting mat. (If you are working with a paper wedge template, fold it in half lengthwise to create a centerline.) Cut along the angled edge to create the initial angle for the strip.

❷ Rotate the ruler so the wide end is on the other side. Align one edge with the cut you just made, and cut along the other side of the ruler. Continue down the strip, rotating the template 180° between each cut.

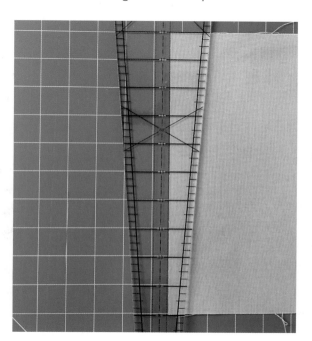

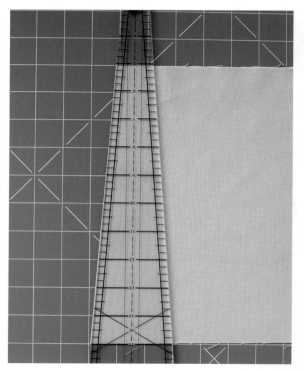

IMPORTANT NOTE *When aligning your template or ruler for in-line or reciprocal cutting, always align the wide end of the wedge you're cutting (or the given measurement on the ruler) with the raw end of the fabric. If you've made minor cutting errors, you may find that the narrow end does not meet the end of the template exactly. That's okay. Aligning the wide end keeps the big end of your wedges consistent, preventing large-scale problems down the road. Inconsistencies at the narrow end of the wedge are easier to adjust for.*

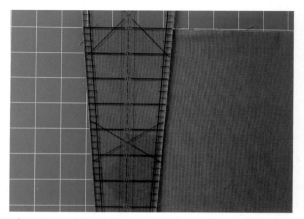

Align the wedge ruler or template using the *wide edge* for each cut.

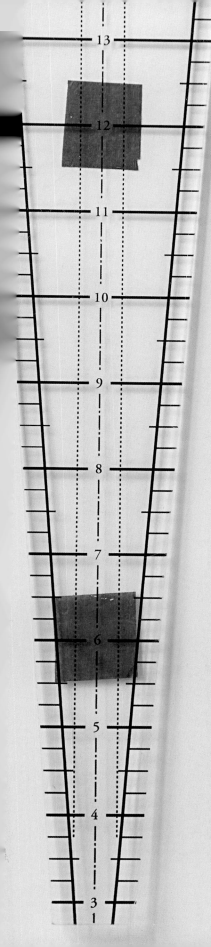

KEEPING YOUR RULER STEADY

Wedge rulers are long and can easily swivel out of place while you are cutting. To keep your ruler steady, follow these tips:

• To minimize shifting, place your hand so that half is on the ruler and half is stabilized on the cutting mat.

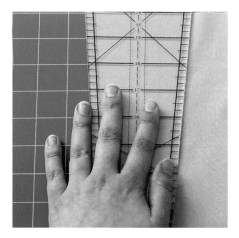

• To make a very long cut, cut the lower part of the wedge; then stop. Keeping the ruler and rotary cutter in place, move your hand higher on the ruler. Complete the cut.

• Use nonslip products designed for quilting templates on the underside of your ruler. As an alternative, place a piece of masking tape on the underside to minimize shifting (*left*).

CUTTING WITH PAPER TEMPLATES AND QUILTING RULERS

Cutting templates for the wedges in this book are supplied on the pattern pullout pages. These templates can be used with wedge rulers or rectangular quilting rulers.

If you have the 9° or 10° wedge ruler called for in the quilt pattern, you can use the supplied templates to find the appropriate spot to align your ruler when cutting wedges. Align the template with the ruler. Note or mark the spot that the top wide edge of the wedge comes to on your ruler. This is the spot you will align with your fabric edge when cutting your wedges.

If you don't have a wedge ruler, you can easily adapt your regular quilting ruler to make use of its straight and sturdy cutting edge.

You will need two copies of the template you wish to use. Be sure to cut them precisely. If the template is small enough, you will be able to fit both copies on one quilting ruler. If you have a large template, you may need two quilting rulers, one for each copy.

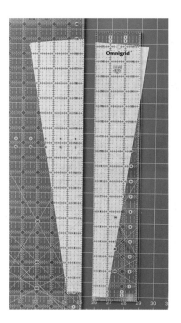

❶ Place the templates so the right edge of one template and the left edge of the other are aligned with a cutting edge of the ruler. Take care to ensure that they are aligned exactly with the edge. Tape them in place. *Fig. A*

❷ Cut the first angle using one of the templates; then switch to the other template, aligning the first cut angle with the template edge under the ruler. Cut along the ruler edge aligned with the template. *Figs. B & C*

❸ Continue switching between the 2 paper templates as you make the cuts.

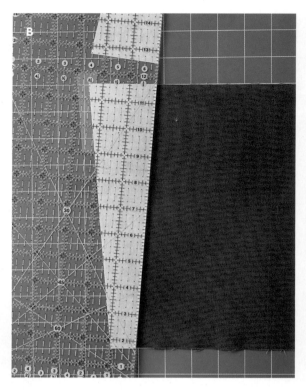

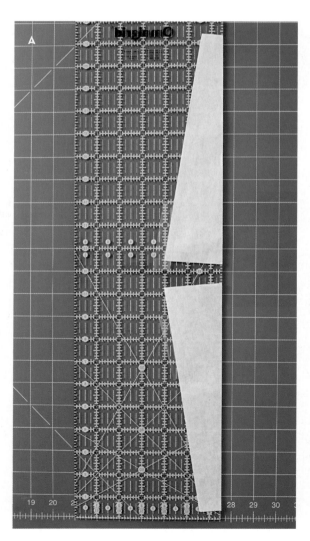

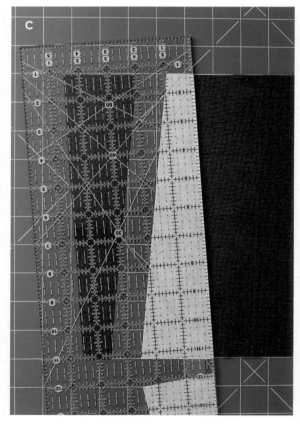

Formulas for Quilt Designers

If you are following my patterns, you won't need to do any calculations. But if you like to design your own quilts, here are the formulas I use when designing mine.

- **For in-line cutting,** you can easily calculate how many wedges can be cut from a strip of fabric. Measure the length of the fabric strip and the width of the wedge's wide end. Divide the fabric length by the wedge width, and round down to the nearest whole number. This is the number of wedges that can be cut from a single strip of fabric.

$$\frac{\text{Length of fabric strip}}{\text{Width of wedge's wide end}} = \text{Number of wedges from strip}$$
(round down to nearest whole number)

- **For reciprocal cutting,** you can also calculate how many wedges can be cut from a strip of fabric, though this calculation is longer. Measure the length of the fabric strip and the width of the wedge's wide end. In addition, measure the wedge's narrow end. Add the wide- and narrow-end measurements together. Divide the length of the fabric strip by this combined measurement. Multiply this number by 2; then subtract 1. Round down to the nearest whole number. This is the number of wedges that can be cut from a single strip of fabric.

$$2\left(\frac{\text{Length of fabric strip}}{\text{Width of wedge's wide end + width of wedge's narrow end}}\right) - 1 = \text{Number of wedges from strip}$$
(round down to nearest whole number)

- **To calculate the size of square that can be cut from a completed wedge round,** measure the diameter (distance across) the completed wedge round. Divide that number by 1.41. The resulting number is the length of the side of the square.

$$\frac{\text{Diameter of completed wedge round}}{1.41} = \text{Length of the square's side}$$

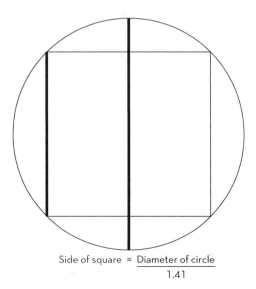

Side of square $= \dfrac{\text{Diameter of circle}}{1.41}$

BASIC ROUND CONSTRUCTION

The most natural thing to do with a wedge ruler is to sew a lot of wedges together into a large circle. And if you've never sewn with wedge shapes before, this is the perfect place to start. You'll get a big piece of patchwork with an impact—and fast!

Wedge Essentials

Here are the details you'll want to know as you're starting:

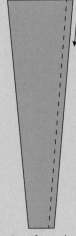

Sew from the wide end to the narrow end.

JOIN YOUR WEDGES STARTING AT THE WIDE END AND WORKING TOWARD THE NARROW END.

This keeps any problems with shifting fabric on the small, manageable edge of your work and keeps the outer edge of your round nicely predictable.

KEEP YOUR ¼" SEAM CONSISTENT.

If you do it the same way every time, you'll have better results. Having a ¼" foot on your sewing machine is incredibly helpful here.

STARCHING FABRIC AND PINNING PIECES WILL HELP, ESPECIALLY IF YOU LIKE PERFECT QUILTS.

Quilters fall on a range of how much imperfection they can stand. If you can't stand any imperfection, pin every seam because your wedges all have bias edges. If you can tolerate some irregularity in your finished piece, you can probably get away with less pinning. I rarely pin before the stage where I join quarter-rounds together, and I'm happy with my results. Pin to your comfort.

Rounds That Behave

If you piece your wedges with a consistent seam allowance and follow the steps below, you will be rewarded with a circle that lies flat. But if you just sew the wedges together, as I did with my first round, you may be disappointed when you sew that last seam.

There are two problems that prevent you from having a flat circle:

• Having a gap once you've pieced all your wedges

• Having an overlap once you've pieced all your wedges

As you can imagine by looking at both of the diagrams (at right), joining the final open seams of the wedge rounds would result in puckers and frustration instead of rounds that lie flat.

These problems start early on in construction, and they may be very slight. For instance, you may let your seam drift by only 1 mm at the narrow tip of your wedges, but if you do that with every seam in a round that contains 40 wedges, you will have 40 mm (over 1½"!) of excess fullness on the inner edge of the round. The round will not lie flat, no matter how long you try to convince it to with your steam iron. As with all piecing, the accuracy of your cutting as well as the accuracy of your ¼" seam will affect your end results.

Even if you are average in your cutting and piecing skills, as I am, it's not a problem getting a round to behave. The secret is in taking the time to square up the piecing before you are at the full-circle stage. Trimming the round at several partial-round stages will allow you to correct inconsistencies in cutting or piecing before they cause you headaches.

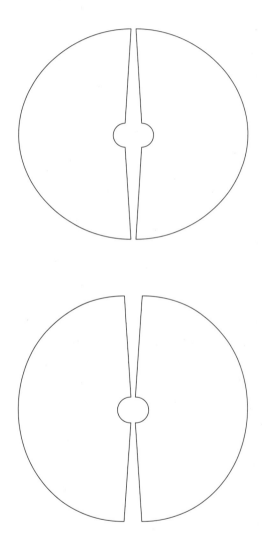

TRIMMING YOUR ROUND AS YOU BUILD IT

Trimming your round in small sections will make it easier for you to bring all the sections together in a full round. I'll never forget the day I realized I had a specialty tool in my sewing room that would allow me to trim my pieces at these stages—my cutting mat! *Fig. A*

My cutting mat (and, I imagine, yours) has 45° marks going in two directions across its surface. These angled lines make a 45° angle with every horizontal and vertical line on the mat. You can use these lines to double-check the angle of the sides of any wedge set that can add up to 45°, such as five wedges cut with a 9° ruler.

When you line up a raw edge of the wedge set with a vertical (or, if you wish, horizontal) line on the cutting mat and the other raw edge of the wedge set with the 45° line, you can see if your edges are true or starting to drift.

You may find that the outer edges are more full than the inner edges or the other way around, with extra fabric on the narrower end that shouldn't be there. Occasionally even I find a bulge in the center, maybe from letting my attention drift mid-seam!

Trimming away these inconsistencies keeps the patchwork on track so it comes together as a nice flat round.

Trimming at the 45° Stage

❶ Press your wedge set (5 wedges if using 9° wedges; 3 wedges if using 15° wedges).

NOTE *I press my seams open when joining wedges. Working this way, I feel that I get a consistent pressed seam, and I also avoid having both seam allowances on one side. Avoiding bulky stacked seam allowances makes it easier to finish the raw edges of the round and makes it easier to quilt over, as well.*

❷ Lay the wedge set on the cutting mat so it aligns as well as possible with the 45° diagonal line on the right side and with a vertical grid line on the left side.

Align so all the fabric comes to the lines but as little fabric as possible extends beyond the lines. *Fig. B*

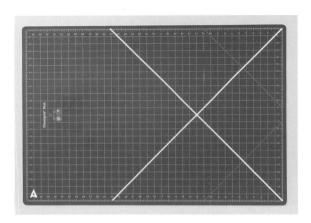

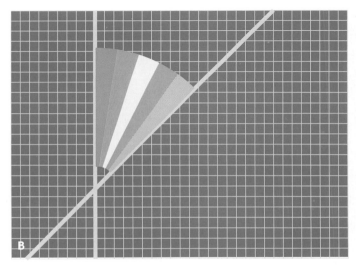

❸ Align your quilting ruler with the 45° diagonal line on the cutting mat, and trim off any fabric that extends beyond the line. Repeat for the vertical line on the other side of the wedge set. *Figs. C & D*

❹ Repeat with the other wedge sets.

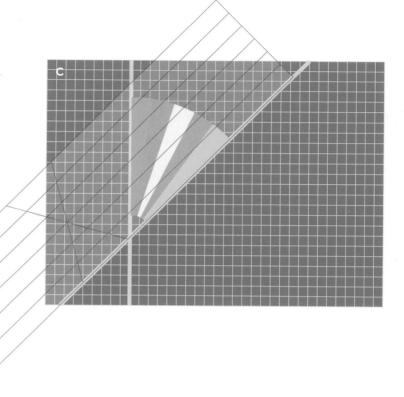

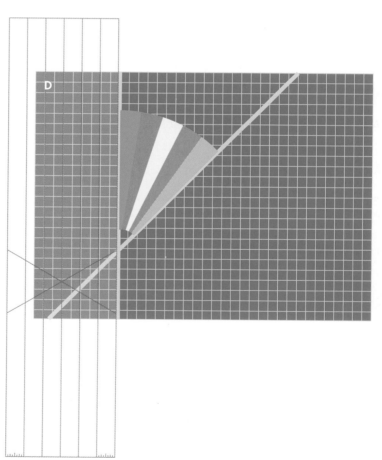

NOTE *The photo at the right shows the risk of skipping the 45° wedge check and waiting to trim until the 90° stage. At the inside of the circle, you can easily identify the narrower wedges that resulted from waiting to trim at the quarter-round stage. If I had trimmed this round earlier, starting with 45° sections (eighth-rounds), my trimming would have been spread over twice as many wedges, and the difference between the trimmed and untrimmed wedges would have been less noticeable.*

Photo by Christina Cameli

Trimming at the 90° Stage

❶ Join the correct number of wedges to make a quarter-round (9 wedges if using 10° wedges; 10 wedges if using 9° wedges). Press.

❷ Align a raw edge of the quarter-round with a vertical line on the cutting mat and the other raw edge with a horizontal line.

❸ Make sure all the fabric comes to the lines and as little as possible extends over.

❹ Align your quilting ruler with the vertical line, and trim the fabric that extends over the line. Repeat for the horizontal line. *Fig. E*

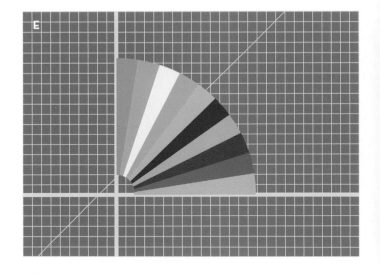

Tip

Trimming 10° Wedges

If you are working with 10° wedges, there is no way to trim at 45°. If your cutting mat has marks for 30° or 60° angles, you can use these lines to trim up wedge sets of 3 or 6 wedges using the same process as trimming at the 45° line. Be sure to trim your wedge sets at the 90° (quarter-round) stage.

Trimming at the Half-Round Stage

If you have taken care to trim at the 90° stage, the rest of the
wedge round usually comes together without difficulty. Join
two quarter-rounds, and make sure they come together to
form a half-round that lies straight on a horizontal line of your
cutting mat. If they don't and you started with square quarter-
rounds, check your last seam; it is likely off. When both sides
of each half-round lie on a straight line, the two halves of the
round then join to make a nice flat round.

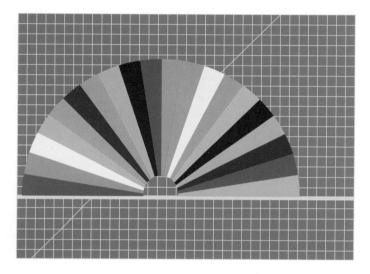

To join the half-rounds, pin the halves together and sew each of
the two remaining seams from the wide end to the narrow end.

Whether you follow the patterns in this book or design your
own wedge rounds, use this basic approach to constructing and
trimming rounds so they come together without headaches.

Finishing the Curved Edges

When you've pieced an entire round together, you can happily marvel at it. Then it's time to deal with the two raw edges—the inner and outer curved edges of the round.

Finish the outside edge of your wedge round using the following techniques:

- Hand appliqué to a background (see Hand Appliqué, page 97).

- Machine appliqué to a background (see Machine Appliqué, page 96).

- Cut the round into a square. If you have several of these, you can piece the squares together, as shown in *Pop Art* (page 74).

- Or you can make a different shape by planning ahead. While you are constructing the round, you can trim away the curved outer edges of each eighth-round, sixth-round, or quarter-round from corner to corner. Piece the sections together to create an octagon, hexagon, or square, respectively. See *The Three of Us* (page 58) and *Prismatic* (page 84).

The inner edge of the wedge round also can be finished in several ways:

- Appliqué something over the opening (page 96). For the projects in this book, you can appliqué a circle just larger than the circle opening using the 7″ center circle pattern (pullout page P1). Or you could appliqué a shape that's not a circle.

- Reverse appliqué by stitching the open circle to a piece of fabric set beneath it (see Skills and Techniques, page 96).

- Piece a set-in circle using freezer paper (see Set-In Circles, page 97).

- If you plan for it while you are constructing the round, you can trim the inner curve to a straight edge at a section stage and add fabric to create an inside point. See *Sea of Serenity* (page 78) and *Prismatic* (page 84) .

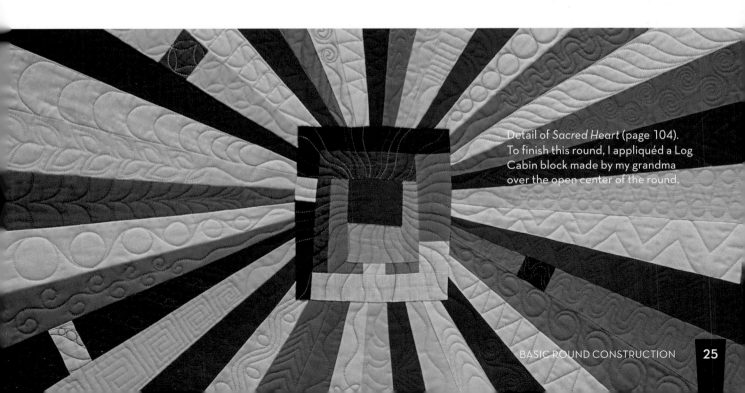

Detail of *Sacred Heart* (page 104). To finish this round, I appliquéd a Log Cabin block made by my grandma over the open center of the round.

HELLO GORGEOUS

43" × 43", designed and made by Christina Cameli, quilted by Nancy Stovall

As this quilt started coming together, I would look at it and think, "Hello, Gorgeous!" Eventually it felt like the quilt was saying the same thing back to me! I love how the radiant wedges bring extra focus to the message. If you're new to wedges, this is a great place to start!

Materials

Yardages are based on 40" usable width, except where noted.

ASSORTED SOLIDS: 12 different fat eighths (9" × 20") for solid wedges

ASSORTED PRINTS, SOLIDS, OR TONE-ON-TONES: Handful of scraps at least 4" in width in each of 6 different colors for pieced wedges

BACKGROUND/CENTER: 1½ yards of 44"-wide fabric

NOTE *In this project, the background square is 43" × 43", so buying background fabric with at least 43" of usable width is critical. If you find the perfect background fabric with less than 43" of usable width, please be aware that you will have less space between the edge of your pieced circle and the edge of the quilt. The pieced circle is 39" in diameter.*

BACKING: 2⅞ yards, pieced to 51" × 51"

BATTING: 51" × 51"

BINDING: ⅜ yard

PERMANENT FABRIC MARKER, such as a Micron Pen

FREEZER PAPER: 7½" × 7½" square

Cutting

Make templates with the 7" center circle pattern and the Hello Gorgeous 9° wedge pattern (pullout page P1), or use a 9° wedge ruler.

ASSORTED SOLIDS

From each fat eighth:

• Cut a rectangle 9" × 17".

Subcut 3 wedges, 36 wedges total. Rotate the template or ruler between cuts, as shown in Reciprocal Cutting (page 14). Fig. A

BACKGROUND/CENTER

• Cut a section 43" × the width of fabric.

Subcut a square 43" × 43".

• Cut a square 8" × 8" for use in the center appliqué.

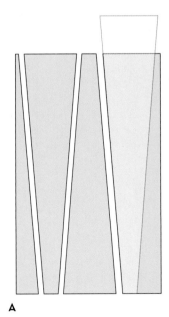

A

Quilt Construction

Refer to Basic Round Construction (page 18) to learn how to construct the circle. Use ¼" seams and press all seams open. Join wedges together from the wide end toward the narrow end.

MAKE SCRAPPY WEDGES

1 Sew color-coordinated scraps together to create 6 pieced strips 4" wide. Press. Trim each strip to 17" in length.

2 From each scrappy strip, cut 1 wedge using the wedge template or ruler. Cut a total of 6 scrappy wedges.

NOTE *You will have 42 wedges to work with, but you will need only 40 for the round. The 2 extra wedges will give you additional design flexibility.*

CONSTRUCT THE WEDGE ROUND

See Rounds That Behave (page 20) to learn how to check and trim your wedge sets at each step: 45°, 90°, and 180°.

1 Arrange 40 wedges in a circle on a table or design wall.

2 When you are satisfied with your design, join the wedges into sets of 5 wedges each. Remember to sew from the wide ends to the narrow ends. Press. You will have 8 wedge sets.

3 Using your cutting mat as a guide, trim each wedge set to 45°.

4 Join the trimmed wedge sets 2 at a time to make 4 quarter-rounds. Press.

5 Using your cutting mat as a guide, align each quarter-round with a horizontal and vertical mark on the cutting mat. Trim as needed to bring each quarter-round to 90°.

6 Join the quarter-rounds in pairs to make 2 half-rounds. Press. Lay the straight raw edges of the half-round along a horizontal line on the cutting mat to make sure the raw edges of the half-round fall along a straight line. Trim as needed.

7 Join the 2 half-rounds to make a full round. Press.

hello
gorgeous

FINISH THE CENTER

❶ Center the 7″ center circle template over the paper side of the freezer paper. Trace the circle shape onto the freezer paper, and cut it out along the drawn line. Place the freezer-paper circle shiny side down on the wrong side of your 8″ × 8″ fabric square for the center round appliqué. Using a warm iron, press the paper side of the freezer paper to adhere it to your fabric. This will stabilize your piece for the next step.

❷ Trim the fabric to the size of the freezer paper circle. Decorate the fabric circle with any words or images you like using the permanent fabric marker. Be sure to keep the design at least ¼″ from the edge to allow for turning under the seam allowance.

❸ Remove the freezer paper by lifting one edge and then pulling. If you need to heat-set your marks, do so now. Turn the center circle face-down, and press the raw edge to the back ¼″.

❹ Place the wedge round right side up on a flat surface. Align the center circle right side up over the open center of the wedge round. Pin in place. Appliqué the center circle down by hand or machine (see Skills and Techniques, page 96).

ASSEMBLE THE QUILT TOP

❶ With the wedge round facedown, press the outer raw edge to the back ¼″.

❷ Find the center of the background fabric by folding it in half in both directions. Mark with a pin. Do the same to the wedge round to find its center. Align the center marks.

If there is an "up" side to your wedge round, be sure it is oriented correctly (not crooked) on the background. Smooth the round out completely so it is not ruffled or folded. Pin the round in place, placing the pins ½″ from the edge of the round.

❸ Appliqué the wedge round to the background fabric by hand or machine.

❹ *Optional:* Turn the piece over. Using small sharp scissors, carefully cut away the excess background fabric from behind the wedge round. Leave a ¼″ seam allowance, and be careful not to cut through the quilt top.

❺ *Optional:* If you would like the quilt to be larger, add borders as desired.

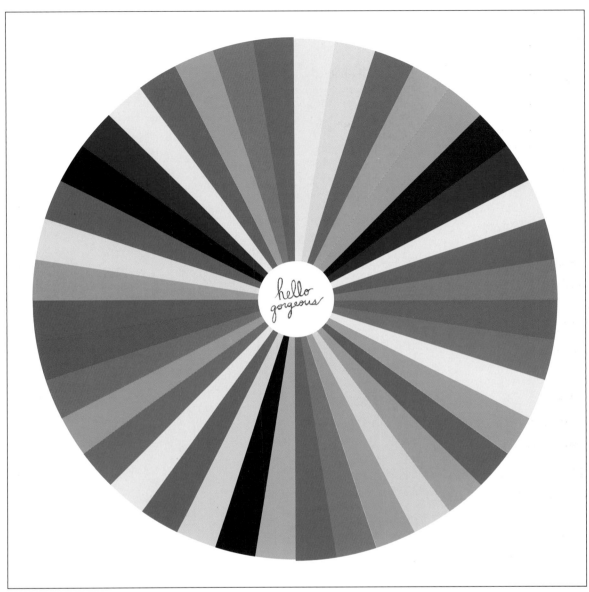

Quilt assembly

FINISH THE QUILT

Layer the backing, batting, and quilt top. Baste and quilt by hand or machine. Then trim and bind!

HALF AND HALF

64" × 83½", designed and made
by Christina Cameli, quilted by Nancy Stovall

Here is a simple way to let your wedges shine—use half-rounds! They stack neatly on top of each other like happy rainbows.

Materials

Yardages are based on 40″ usable width, except where noted.

ASSORTED PRINTS:
20 fat quarters for arcs

BACKGROUND: 4 yards
of 42″-wide fabric

BACKING: 5¼ yards,
pieced to 72″ × 92″

BATTING: 72″ × 92″

BINDING: ½ yard

NOTE *If your background fabric has at least 42″ of usable width, you will be able to piece the 83½″ background with only 2 widths of fabric. With narrower fabric, you will need extra to make your background large enough.*

Cutting

Make a template with the Half and Half 9° wedge pattern (pullout page P1), or use a 9° wedge ruler.

ASSORTED PRINTS

From each fat quarter:

• Cut 3 strips 5″ × 20″.

   Layer the strips and subcut wedges, 480 total. Rotate the template or ruler between cuts, as shown in Reciprocal Cutting (page 14).

BACKGROUND

• Cut 2 rectangles 42″ × 64″.

Quilt Construction

Refer to Basic Round Construction (page 18) to learn how to construct the half-rounds. Use ¼″ seams and press all seams open. Join wedges together from the wide end toward the narrow end.

CREATING THE ARCS

See Rounds That Behave (page 20) to learn how to check and trim your wedge sets at each step: 45°, 90°, and 180°.

❶ Join wedges randomly in sets of 5 wedges each. Press. Make 96 wedge sets.

❷ Trim each wedge set using the 45° mark on your cutting mat.

❸ Join the wedge sets in pairs to make 48 quarter-rounds. Press.

❹ Trim each quarter-round to 90° using the marks on your cutting mat.

❺ Set aside 8 quarter-rounds. Join the remaining quarter-rounds in pairs to make 20 half-rounds. Press.

MAKING THE BACKGROUND

Join the 42″ × 64″ pieces together along the long edges to make a large rectangle 64″ × 83½″.

ASSEMBLE THE QUILT TOP

❶ With a half-round facedown, press the raw edges of the inner and outer curve to the back ¼″. Repeat with all half-rounds and quarter-rounds.

❷ Find and mark the center of the top edge of the background.

❸ Align the center of a half-round with the marked center, 2″ below the top edge of the background. Add half-rounds on either side of the center half-round, keeping the top of each round 2″ from the top edge of the background. The outer curves of the rounds should just touch at the bottom edge. Pin the 3 half-rounds in place. *Fig. A*

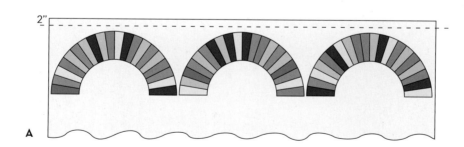

2″

A

4 Using a topstitch needle and coordinating thread, appliqué the half-rounds in place using a straight stitch.

5 Align the next row—2 half-rounds and 2 quarter-rounds—by first aligning the half-rounds so they cover the bottom of the previous row's half-rounds by ⅛". Pin in place. Don't worry about the precise distance between the tops of the rounds; I included extra background fabric at the bottom of the quilt to accommodate variations in the vertical distance between the arcs. *Fig. B*

6 Pin quarter-rounds next to the half-rounds. The ¼" seam allowance of the quarter-rounds may extend beyond the edge of the background on the sides. *Fig. C*

7 Using a ruler, check that the bottom edges of your half- and quarter-rounds are the same distance from the top of the background to avoid the row slanting unintentionally. Appliqué the pieces in place.

8 Continue to add rows, alternating each row of 3 half-rounds with a row of 2 half-rounds and 2 quarter-rounds. Appliqué as you go until you have made 8 rows.

9 If your final row of rounds does not extend all the way to the bottom edge of your background fabric, trim the remaining background fabric away, taking care to keep the bottom edge square with the sides of the quilt top. Sew the strip cut from the bottom to the top edge of the quilt.

B

C

Quilt assembly. Trim any excess at the lower edge, and add it to the top edge.

FINISH THE QUILT

Layer the backing, batting, and quilt top. Baste and quilt by hand or machine.
Then trim and bind!

ROUND VARIATIONS

There is tremendous freedom in using wedge shapes
to create dynamic design. Here are some possibilities for you to try.

Scrappy Wedges

Whether your goal is a little interruption somewhere along the wedge or an all-out scrap-tastic celebration, cutting single wedges from patchwork gives you a chance to customize a quilt pattern and use up beloved scraps!

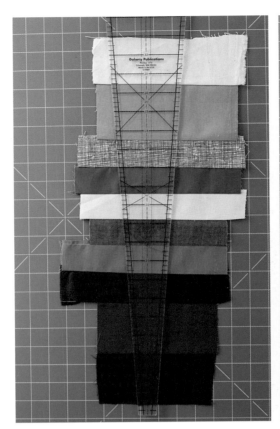
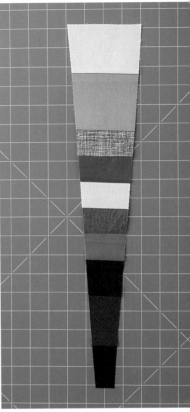

Rounds That Use Gradient Fabric

Using fabric that shifts from one color to another gives a sense of movement to wedge rounds. To cut gradient fabric or other directional fabric, use in-line cutting (page 13).

Pointed Wedges

To add points to a round, fold the round in half lengthwise, right sides together. Use a ¼″ seam to stitch the wide end from the fold to the open edge. Turn right side out and press. Then join the wedges in the usual fashion.

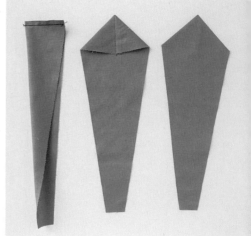

Rounds with Pieced Strips

Your designs can become more complex by cutting your wedges from strip sets. Experiment with different approaches. Try coloring a strip set on paper and cutting wedge shapes from it to see what you get. To keep the pattern the same in each wedge, use in-line cutting (page 13).

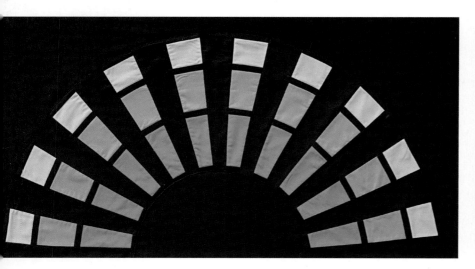
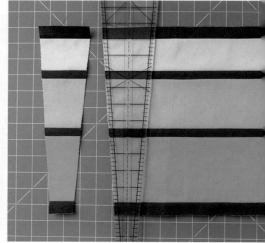

Rounds with Inverted Pieced Strips

Wedges cut in a reciprocal manner from strip sets (page 14) typically create an interesting design when placed together. This effect can be highlighted with bold color placement.

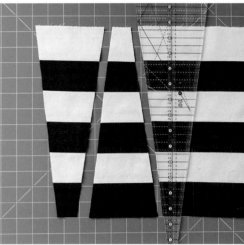

Slanted Wedges

Cutting wedges at an angle from strip sets creates a pointed, pieced end to each wedge. Many wedge rulers have lines to keep the angle of the cut consistent from one cut to the next. If yours doesn't, you can use a strip of tape applied to the underside of the ruler to be your guide. Align the guide with a seam or the raw edge of the fabric for each cut.

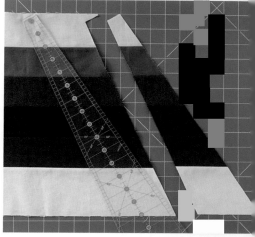

Rounds That Use More Than One Size of Wedge

With any wedge ruler, you can use two wedges of the same length cut at different spots on the ruler, alternating them big and small. They will still come together in a circular fashion.

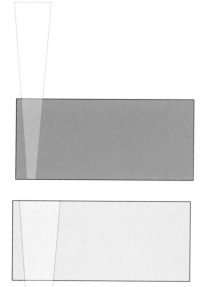

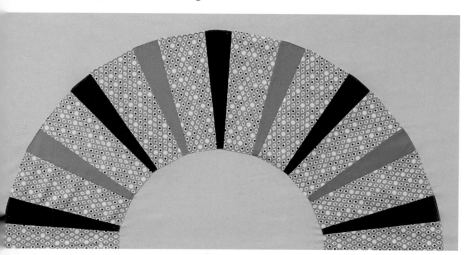

Rounds That Use Inserted Strips

Adding a strip to the side of a wedge will make space between that wedge and the next. The sewn unit will still maintain the same angle as the original wedge. A circle sewn in this manner will be larger than if it was sewn without inserted strips.

Detail of *Sparkler* (page 52)

GOOD NIGHT,
GOOD MORNING

65″ × 83½″, designed and made
by Christina Cameli, quilted by Nancy Stovall

This scrap-friendly quilt is for the little sunshine you spend your days with and the little love you tuck in at night.

Materials

Yardages are based on 40″ usable width.

"Sun" side

MEDIUM BLUE: 3 yards for background

YELLOW/ORANGE SCRAPS: 10 pieces 7″ × the width of fabric or smaller for wedges (See Sun and Moon Scraps, page 46, for sizes.)

"Moon" side

DARK BLUE: 3 yards for background

WHITE/LIGHT BLUE SCRAPS: 10 pieces 7″ × the width of fabric or smaller for wedges (See Sun and Moon Scraps, page 46, for sizes.)

Center circle

LIGHT BLUE AND YELLOW: 1 rectangle at least 4¼″ × 8″ of each

Other

BACKING: 5¼ yards, pieced to 73″ × 92″

BATTING: 73″ × 92″

BINDING: ⅓ yard *each* of both background fabrics

FREEZER PAPER

Cutting

Make templates with the 6¾″ set-in circle pattern (pullout page P2) and the full 9° wedge pattern (pullout page P1), or use a 9° wedge ruler.

BACKGROUND FABRICS

For each of the pieces listed below, cut from the sun background fabric (medium blue) and the moon background fabric (dark blue).

For the background:

• Cut a rectangle 42″ × 65″ from each background fabric and set aside.

For the background wedges:

• Cut 1 strip 22½″ × the width of fabric from each background fabric. See Make the Background Wedges (page 48) for subcutting instructions.

For the strip-pieced wedges:

• Cut 1 strip 1¾″ × the width of fabric from each background fabric.

  From each strip, subcut 4 rectangles 1¾″ × 5″: 2 for strip sets C and 2 for strip sets E.

• From the remaining fabric, cut the following from each background fabric:

  1 rectangle 1½″ × 15″ for strip set A

  1 rectangle 2″ × 20″ for strip set B

  2 rectangles 1″ × 30″ for strip sets C

  2 rectangles 1¼″ × 25″ for strip sets D

  2 rectangles 1½″ × 35″ for strip sets E

  2 rectangles 1″ × 40″ and 2 rectangles 1″ × 10″ for strip sets F

Cutting continues on next page.

SUN AND MOON SCRAPS

For the strip-pieced wedges:

Cut 2 sets of the rectangles listed below: 1 from the sun scraps (yellow/orange) and 1 from the moon scraps (white/light blue). If 2 rectangles are listed, make them from different fabrics within the sun or moon color group.

- Cut 1 rectangle 7″ × 15″ for strip set A.

- Cut 1 rectangle 4½″ × 20″ for strip set B.

- Cut 2 rectangles 3½″ × 30″ for strip sets C.

- Cut 2 rectangles 4¼″ × 25″ for strip sets D.

- Cut 2 rectangles 2½″ × 35″ for strip sets E.

- Cut 2 rectangles 2¼″ × 40″ and 2 rectangles 2¼″ × 10″ for strip sets F.

Quilt Construction

Refer to Basic Round Construction (page 18) to learn how to construct the circle. Use ¼″ seams and press all seams open. Join wedges together from the wide end toward the narrow end.

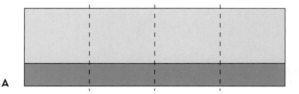

A

MAKE THE STRIP-PIECED WEDGES

❶ Make strip sets by joining each sun or moon wedge rectangle with the matching background rectangle from its colorway. From each color-way, you will have 1 strip set A and B and 2 strip sets C, D, E, and F. Subcut 5″ pieced segments from each set. *Fig. A*

❷ Join the segments from each strip set together to create long strip units 5″ wide, with the fabrics alternating between sun or moon wedge rectangles and background rectangles.

❸ To extend strip units C and E, add an extra 1¾″ × 5″ background rectangle to the sun or moon end of the strip unit so the strip unit begins and ends with a background rectangle.

❹ From each pieced strip set, cut 1 wedge. Always align the wide end of the wedge template with a strip of the background fabric. *Fig. B*

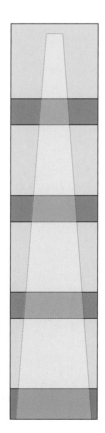

B

Make the Background Wedges

❶ From the 22½″ medium blue strip, cut 12 wedges. Rotate the template or ruler between cuts, as shown in Reciprocal Cutting (page 14). From the 22½″ dark blue strip, cut 11 wedges. Set aside 10 medium blue wedges and 9 dark blue wedges to use in the pieced round.

❷ Fold the 2 remaining medium-blue background wedges in half lengthwise, wrong sides together, and press to create a centerline.

❸ Open the pressed wedges. Place each pressed medium blue wedge on top of a dark-blue background wedge, right sides together and with the edges aligned. Stitch along the pressed centerline.

❹ Trim away the excess fabric ¼″ to the right of the stitched line on one set and ¼″ to the left of the stitched line on the second set. Press the compound wedges open. *Figs. A–D*

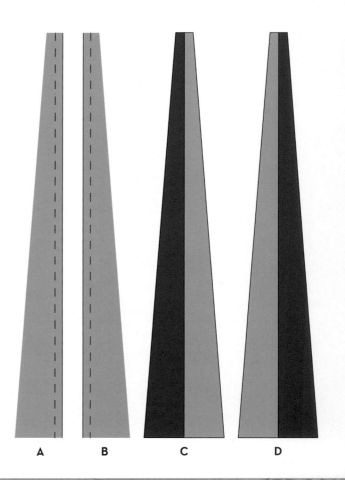

A   B   C   D

CREATE THE ROUND

See Rounds That Behave (page 20) to learn how to check and trim your wedge sets at each step: 45°, 90°, and 180°.

❶ Arrange the wedges to create the sun and moon halves of the quilt, alternating pieced and background wedges. Place the 2 compound wedges on opposite sides of the circle to create a horizon line between night and day.

❷ Choose 1 sun wedge to be extended from the circle. Set it aside to be appliquéd to the quilt top after you have attached the completed round to the background fabric. In its place, substitute the additional medium-blue background wedge. *Fig. E*

❸ Join the wedges into sets of 5 wedges each. Press. *Fig. F*

❹ Use the 45° marking on your cutting mat to trim the wedge sets.

❺ Join pairs of trimmed wedge sets to make quarter-rounds. Press. Use the perpendicular lines on your cutting mat to trim the quarter-rounds.

❻ Join pairs of quarter-rounds to make 2 half-rounds. Press.

❼ Join the half-rounds to make a full round.

E

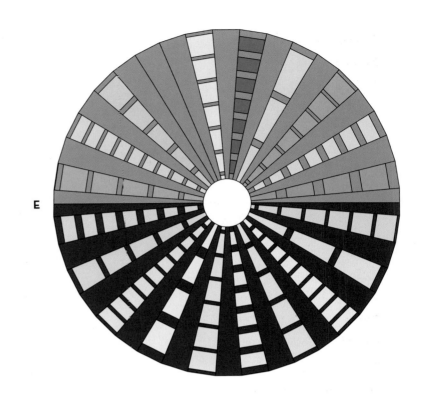

F

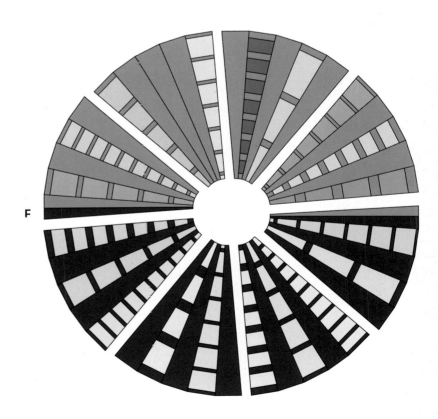

FINISH THE CENTER

❶ Join the center circle rectangles along an 8″ side to make an 8″ square. Press.

❷ Use the 6¾″ set-in circle template to attach the inner circle to the round. Be sure to align the yellow half of the square with the "sun" side of the round and the light blue half of the square with the "moon" side of the round. The center seam should align with the seams in the half-and-half wedges. Refer to Set-In Circles (page 97).

ATTACH THE ROUND

❶ Remove the selvages from the 65″ sections of medium and dark blue fabrics. Join the fabrics along the 65″ edges, and trim to create a 65″ × 83½″ background.

❷ With the round right side down, press the raw outer edge to the back ¼″.

❸ Right sides up, place the round on top of the pieced background, taking care to align the background seam with the seams of the compound wedges. Pin the round in place, and appliqué it with your preferred method. Refer to Machine Appliqué (page 96) or Hand Appliqué (page 97).

❹ Flip the quilt top over, and carefully trim away the background that is covered by the round.

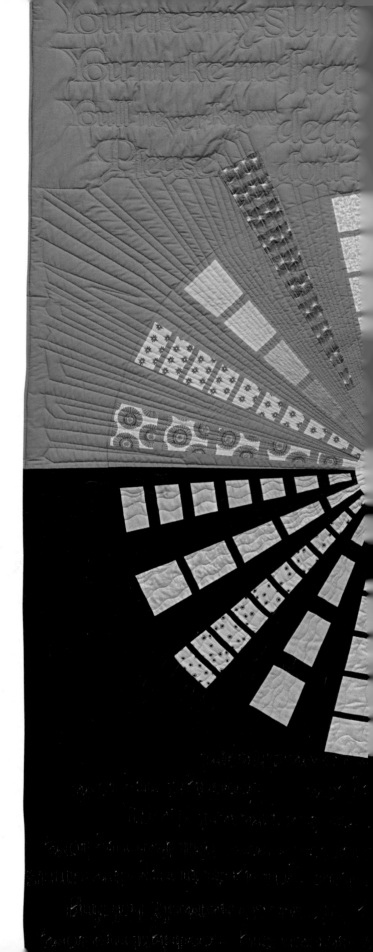

ATTACH THE EXTRA WEDGE

❶ Press a ¼″ seam allowance to the back around each side of the pieced sun wedge you set aside in Create the Round, Step 2 (page 49).

❷ Align the wedge as desired on the quilt top, and pin it in place.

❸ Appliqué using your preferred method.

FINISH THE QUILT

Layer the backing, batting, and quilt top. Baste and quilt by hand or machine. Then trim and bind!

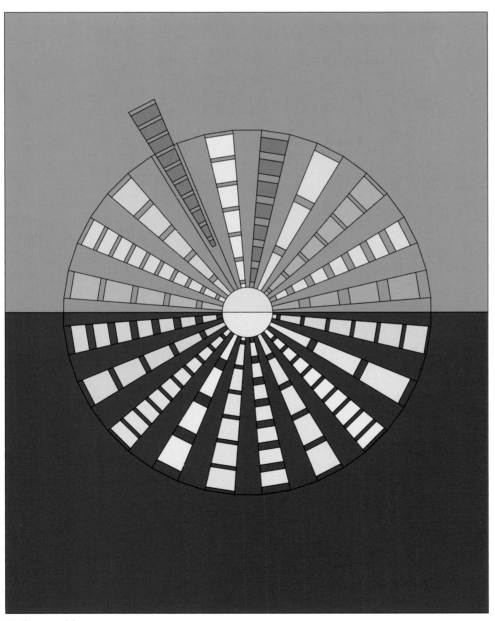

Quilt assembly

SPARKLER

56" diameter; designed, made, and
quilted by Christina Cameli

Here's a dynamic quilt that borders on chaos. If you don't want it to be round, you can mount it onto a background using the process described in HELLO GORGEOUS (page 26).

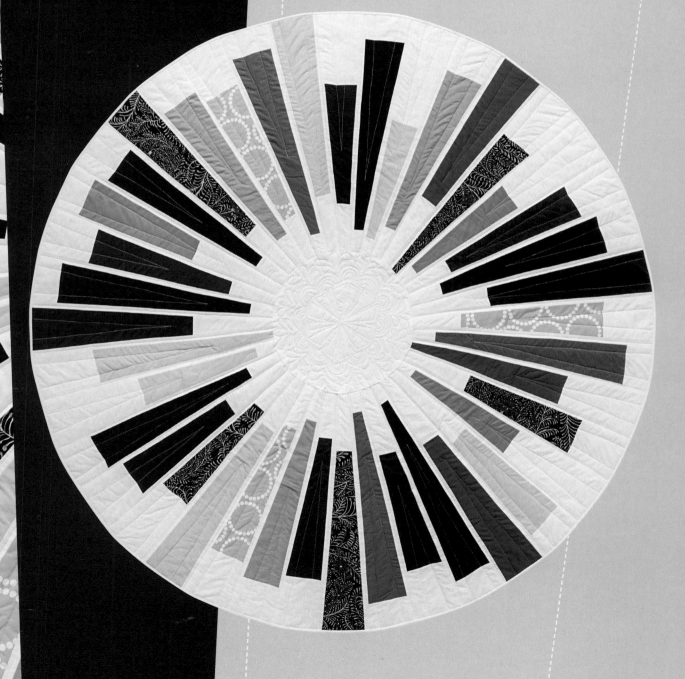

Materials

Yardages are based on 40" usable width.

ASSORTED COLOR FABRICS:
14 fat quarters or scraps
10" × 18" (no more than
2 scraps from any 1 fabric)

BACKGROUND: 2¼ yards

BACKING: 3⅝ yards,
pieced to 64" × 64"

BATTING: 64" × 64"

BINDING: ⅜ yard

Cutting

Make a template with the full 9° wedge pattern (pullout page P1), or use a 9° wedge ruler.

BACKGROUND

• Cut 28 strips 1" × the width
  of fabric.

  From each strip, subcut
  1 rectangle 1" × 22½" and
  1 rectangle 1" × 11½" to add
  to the sides of the wedges.

• Cut 3 strips 10" × the width
  of fabric.

  Subcut the rectangles listed in
  the Strip Sets chart (at right).

• Cut 1 square 15" × 15"
  to reverse appliqué to the
  center circle.

ASSORTED COLOR FABRICS

Using the fat quarters and the 10" background strips you cut,
follow the chart to cut rectangles for the strip sets.

Strip Sets

For each strip set, cut *2 sets* of the following. To avoid too many
similar-looking wedges in the quilt, do not use the same-color fabric
for identical strip sets.

Strip set	From the color fabric	From the 10" background strips
A	1 rectangle 10" × 18"	2 rectangles 10" × 2¾"
B	1 rectangle 10" × 13½"	2 rectangles 10" × 5"
C	1 rectangle 10" × 17"	1 rectangle 10" × 6"
D	1 rectangle 10" × 15¼"	1 rectangle 10" × 7¾"
E	1 rectangle 10" × 11½"	1 rectangle 10" × 2¾" 1 rectangle 10" × 9¼"
F	1 rectangle 10" × 16"	2 rectangles 10" × 3¾"
G	1 rectangle 10" × 11½"	1 rectangle 10" × 7" 1 rectangle 10" × 5"

Quilt Construction

Refer to Basic Round Construction (page 18) to learn how to construct the circle. Use ¼″ seams and press all seams open. Join wedges together from the wide end toward the narrow end.

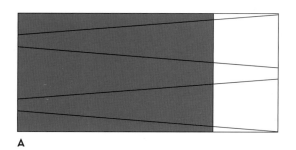

A

MAKE THE STRIP SETS

Using the pieces listed in the cutting chart, piece together each strip set along the 10″ sides for a total of 14 strip sets. When there are 2 background rectangles in the set, place the print between the 2 backgrounds. Use a short stitch length, as these strip sets will be subcut. The finished size of each strip set should be 10″ × 22½″.

CUT THE WEDGES

From each pieced strip set, cut 3 wedges, 42 total. Rotate the template or ruler between cuts, as shown in Reciprocal Cutting (page 14). *Figs. A & B*

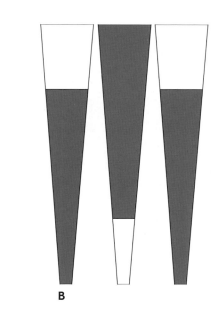

B

ADD BACKGROUND STRIPS TO THE WEDGES

❶ Join the 1″ × 11½″ background rectangles in pairs end to end to make 14 rectangles 1″ × 22½″. Press. You should now have 42 rectangles 1″ × 22½″—some pieced, some not.

NOTE *Are you wondering why I didn't ask you to cut 14 more rectangles 1″ × 22½″ instead of asking you to cut 2 shorter pieces and join them together? This method saves fabric since you can't cut 2 strips 22½″ in length from 1 width of fabric. You can cut a 22½″ strip and an 11½″ strip from 1 width, though, which lets you use the fabric that might have otherwise been set aside.*

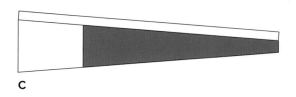

C

❷ Join a 1″ × 22½″ background rectangle to the right edge of a wedge. Repeat to make 42 wedge/strip units. Press. Trim the edges even with the wedge if needed. *Fig. C*

CONSTRUCT THE ROUND

See Rounds That Behave (page 20) to learn how to check and trim your wedge sets at each step: 45°, 90°, and 180°.

❶ Arrange the wedge/strip units to create your preferred layout. Use only 40 wedges. You have 2 extra wedges to allow for design flexibility and substitution.

❷ Sew the wedge/strip units together in sets of 5. Press. Using the 45° angle on your cutting mat, trim each section to 45°.

❸ Join the sections in pairs to create quarter-rounds. Press. Use the perpendicular lines on your cutting mat to trim to 90°.

❹ Join the quarter-rounds to create half-rounds. Join the half-rounds and press.

Quilt assembly

FINISH THE CENTER

❶ Turn the seam allowance of the inner circle to the back ¼", pressing as you go.

❷ Pin the 15" × 15" background square underneath the open inner circle.

❸ Appliqué the inner circle edge to the background by hand or machine (page 96).

FINISH THE QUILT

Layer the backing, batting, and quilt top. Baste and quilt by hand or machine. Then trim and bind! Bias binding works best for curved pieces such as this.

Tip

If you would like to finish your quilt as a square, piece a background 60" × 60" and appliqué the circle to the background by hand or machine (page 96).

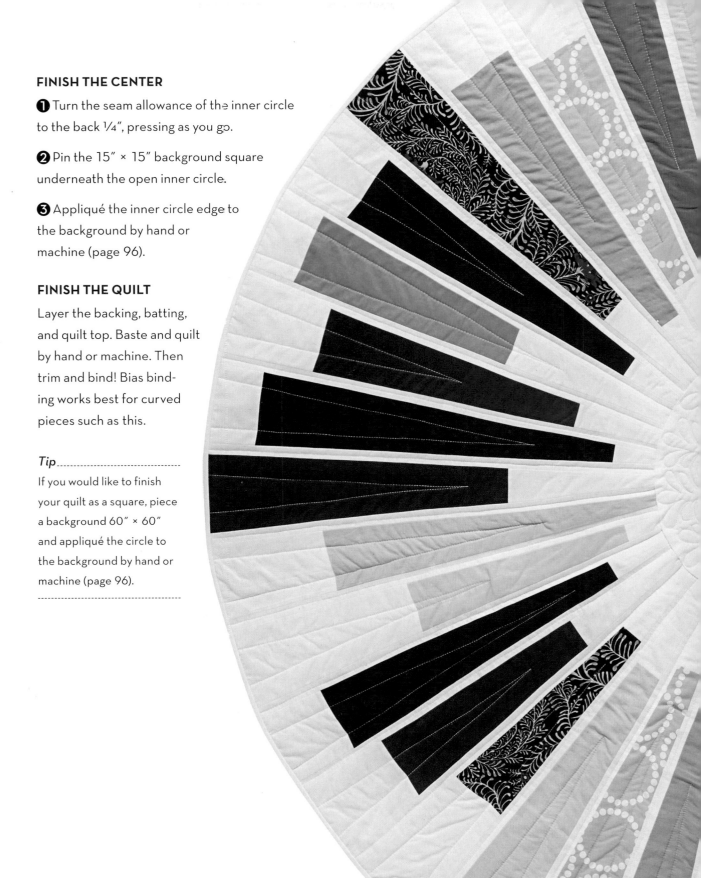

THE THREE OF US

79½" × 84½", designed and made by Christina Cameli, quilted by Nancy Stovall

With their colors carefully arranged, wedges can create spinning wheels like these: a mama and her two babies to my eyes! Trimming the wedge sets at the 45° stage makes it possible to finish the round by piecing it as an octagon.

Materials

Yardages are based on 40" usable width, except where noted.

Assign Color A to the largest wedge of the wheel, Color B to the next largest, and so on.

COLOR A: 1 yard

COLOR B: 7/8 yard

COLOR C: 3/4 yard

COLOR D: 5/8 yard

COLOR E: 1/2 yard

BACKGROUND: 6½ yards of 44"-wide fabric

NOTE If your background fabric has at least 44" of usable width, you will be able to cut 4 rectangles from a strip 8½" × the width of fabric, as described in Extra 11" Background Strips (page 60). If your favorite background fabric isn't wide enough, buy an extra 1/3 yard.

BACKING: 7⅓ yards, pieced to 88" × 93"

BATTING: 88" × 93"

BINDING: 5/8 yard

FREEZER PAPER

Cutting

Make templates with the 6¾" set-in circle pattern (pullout page P2), the full 9° wedge pattern (pullout page P1), and The Three of Us small 9° wedge pattern (pullout page P1), or use a 9° wedge ruler.

STRIP SETS FOR WEDGES

Mark the color and background strips by letter, and keep the sets together to avoid confusion.

Large Wheel

Cut 1 strip in the size indicated × the width of fabric in each wedge color.

Fabric	Wedge color				
	A	**B**	**C**	**D**	**E**
Background (outer edge)	—	4¾"	8"	11¼"	14½"
Colors	16"	13¼"	11½"	10"	8½"
Background (inner edge)	7"	5½"	4"	2¼"	—

Cutting continues on next page.

Small Wheels

From the background fabrics, cut 1 strip in the size indicated × the width of fabric. In addition, you will need a background strip in the size indicated × 11". See Cutting Extra 11" Background Strips (below) for cutting instructions for the 11" lengths.

From the color fabrics, cut 2 strips the size indicated × the width of fabric. Subcut the second strip to 11".

Fabric	Wedge color				
	A	**B**	**C**	**D**	**E**
Background (outer edge)	—	2½"	4½"	6½"	8½"
Color	9½"	8¼"	7"	5¾"	4½"
Background (inner edge)	3½"	2¾"	2"	1¼"	—

EXTRA 11" BACKGROUND STRIPS

From the background fabric:

• Cut 1 strip 8½" × the width of fabric.

Subcut 4 rectangles 8½" × 11". Set aside 1 rectangle for wedge E in the Small Wheels cutting chart (above).

Following the diagrams below, subcut the remaining 3 rectangles lengthwise to create 11" strips for the remaining wedges in the cutting chart for the small wheels. *Figs. A–C*

GENERAL CUTTING

From the background fabric:

• Cut 1 strip 14½" × the width of fabric.

Subcut 2 squares 14½" × 14½". Cut each square in half once diagonally to create 4 triangles. These are the background triangles to finish the large octagons.

• Cut 1 strip 9¼" × the width of fabric.

Subcut 4 squares 9¼" × 9¼". Cut each square in half once diagonally to create 8 triangles. These are the background triangles to finish the small octagons.

• Cut 1 strip 8" × the width of fabric.

Subcut 3 squares 8" × 8" for the block centers.

• See Assemble the Quilt Top (page 64) for the remaining cutting instructions.

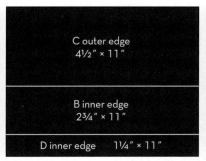

B outer edge
2½" × 11"

A inner edge
3½" × 11"

scrap

A

C outer edge
4½" × 11"

B inner edge
2¾" × 11"

D inner edge   1¼" × 11"

B

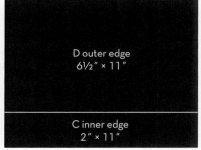

D outer edge
6½" × 11"

C inner edge
2" × 11"

C

Quilt Construction

Refer to Basic Round Construction (page 18) to learn how to construct the circles. Use ¼" seams and press all seams open. Join wedges together from the wide end toward the narrow end.

MAKE STRIP SETS

❶ Join the background and color strips to make strip sets as described in the Large Wheel chart. You will have 5 large strip sets. With strip set B, mark which end is for the outer edge—the inner-edge and outer-edge widths are easily confused. Use a short stitch length, as these strip sets will be subcut.

❷ For the small wheels, join the long background and color strips to make 5 strip sets, and join the 11" background and color strips to make 5 strip sets. With the B strip sets, mark which end is for the outer edge—the inner-edge and outer-edge widths are easily confused.

CUT WEDGES FOR THE WHEELS

❶ From each of the large strip sets, cut 8 wedges using the full wedge template, aligning the wide end of the template with the outer edge of the background strip.

❷ From each of the small strip sets, cut 16 wedges using the small wedge template, aligning the wide end of the wedge with the outer edge of the background strip.

MAKE THE OCTAGONS

See Rounds That Behave (page 20) to learn how to check and trim your wedge sets at each step: 45°, 90°, and 180°.

❶ Join the wedges in sets of 5 in the order D, E, A, B, and C, as shown. You will have 8 large wedge sets and 16 small wedge sets. Press. Using the 45° lines on your cutting mat, trim each wedge set as needed. *Fig. A*

❷ Trim each wedge set from corner to corner at the wide end. *Fig. B*

❸ Join pairs of wedge sections to make quarter-octagons. Press. Use the perpendicular lines on your cutting mat to trim as needed (page 23).

❹ Join the quarter-octagons to make half-octagons. Press.

❺ Join the half-octagons to make 1 large octagon and 2 small octagons. The large octagon should measure 47" × 47", and the small octagon should measure 28½" × 28½". *Fig. C*

FINISH THE OCTAGONS

❶ Find the center of the long edge of each large background triangle by folding it in half. Finger-press.

❷ On the large octagon, find the center of each corner wedge by folding it in half. Finger-press.

❸ Match the marked spots and pin. Join a triangle to each diagonal edge to form a square. Press. *Fig. D*

❹ Repeat Steps 1–3 using the small background triangles and the small octagons.

❺ If the triangle extends beyond the straight edges of the octagon, trim it even with the octagon as necessary. *Fig. E*

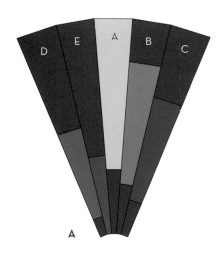

A

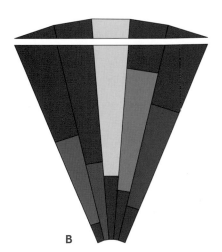

B

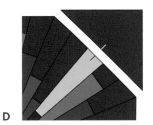

D

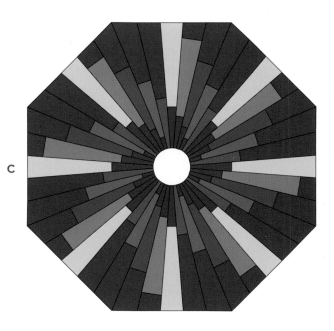

C

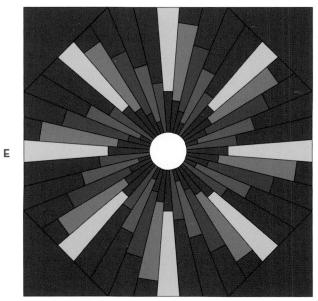

E

Wedge assembly

FINISH THE BLOCK CENTERS

Finish the inner circles of each octagon using the set-in circle technique. Refer to Set-In Circles (page 97) and the 6¾" set-in circle template (pattern pullout page P2).

ASSEMBLE THE QUILT TOP

❶ Cut the remaining background fabric as follows (*Fig. F*):

• For pieces AA and BB, cut 2 strips 3" × the width of fabric.

Piece the strips end to end, and subcut them to 3" × 47" (AA) and 3" × 28½" (BB).

• For piece CC, cut a strip 19" × the width of fabric.

Subcut 1 rectangle 19" × 28½".

• For piece DD, cut a 21½" strip × the width of fabric.

Subcut 1 rectangle 21½" × 31".

• For piece EE, cut a 28½" strip × the width of fabric.

Subcut 1 rectangle 28½" × 31".

• For the upper border, cut 2 strips 3" × the width of fabric.

• For the bottom border, cut 2 strips 5" × the width of fabric.

• For the side borders, cut 4 strips 1½" × the width of fabric.

❷ Sew rectangle AA to the bottom of the large wheel. Press.

❸ Sew rectangle CC to the left side of a small wheel. Press.

❹ Sew the small wheel unit from Step 3 to the bottom of the large wheel unit from Step 2. Press. Set this unit aside while you work on the right half of the quilt top.

❺ Sew rectangle BB to the left side of the remaining small wheel. Press.

❻ Sew rectangle DD to the top of the small wheel unit from Step 5. Press.

❼ Sew rectangle EE to the bottom of the small wheel unit from Step 6. Press.

❽ Sew the large wheel unit from Step 4 to the left side of the unit from Step 7. Press.

Add Borders

❶ Sew the 3" strips for the top border end to end. Press.

❷ Sew the 5" strips for the bottom border end to end. Press.

❸ Measure the width of the quilt. Trim the pieced border strips from Steps 1 and 2 to this measurement, and sew them to the top and bottom of the quilt.

❹ Sew the 1½" side border strips in pairs. Press.

❺ Measure the length of the quilt. Trim the pieced side border strips to this measurement, and sew one to each side of the quilt.

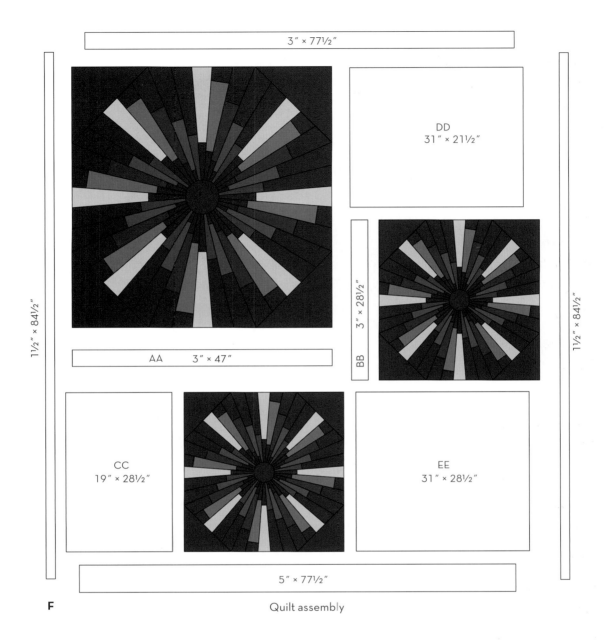

3" × 77½"

DD
31" × 21½"

1½" × 84½"

BB   3" × 28½"

1½" × 84½"

AA   3" × 47"

CC
19" × 28½"

EE
31" × 28½"

5" × 77½"

F

Quilt assembly

FINISH THE QUILT

Layer the backing, batting, and quilt top. Baste and quilt by hand or machine. Then trim and bind!

BEYOND ROUNDS

While rounds can keep you busy for a long time, they are only part of the wedge story. This chapter shows you a number of quilts that depart from the circular structure for a new wedge experience altogether.

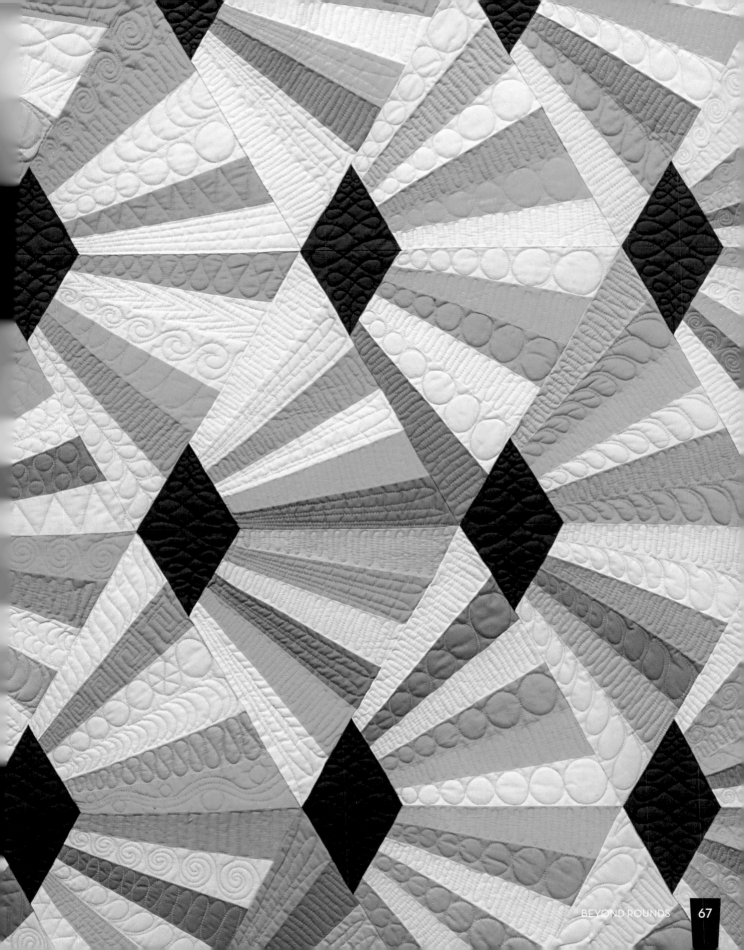

IT TAKES ALL SORTS

48½" × 66"; designed,
made, and quilted by Christina Cameli

One easy way to play with wedges is to join them in strips, alternating their wide ends. Even when wedges are different widths, they will work together just fine to create straight strips if they are all cut with the same-degree ruler. Here I take this flexibility to the lovely linen clothing left behind after my grandma's passing to create exactly the sort of quilt she would have loved—harmonious without being predictable or fussy.

Materials

Yardages are based on 40" usable width.

SCRAPS: 8½" strips in a variety of fabrics. You will need about 450" of 8½" strips in various widths to cut the wedges for this quilt.

BACKING: 3¼ yards, pieced to 57" × 74"

BATTING: 57" × 74"

BINDING: ½ yard

Cutting

Make a template with the It Takes All Sorts *full 10° wedge pattern (pullout page P1), or use a 10° wedge ruler.*

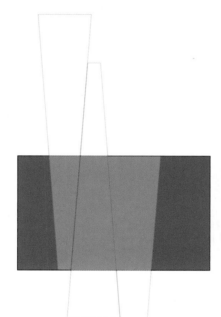

• Cut all scraps to 8½" to get a uniform wedge length.

• Using the wedge template, cut 210 wedges from the scraps. Vary the placement of the ruler on the scraps to create wedges in different widths.

Quilt Construction

Use ¼" seams and press all seams open.

MAKE THE PIECED WEDGES

❶ Join a few wedges in alternating directions to make a piece at least 8½" × 8½".

Tip ···

When joining your wedges, offset the pieces slightly to match up the ¼" stitching line at the top and bottom of the wedges. For more on aligning angled pieces, see Sewing Angled Pieces Accurately (page 100).

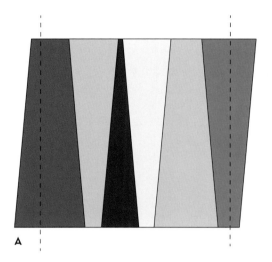

A

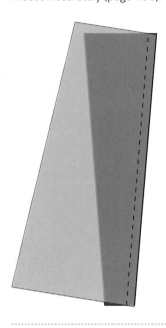

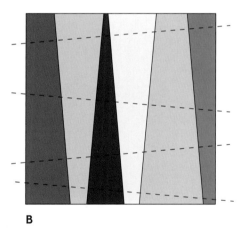

B

❷ Trim to 8½" wide. *Fig. A*

❸ Using the wedge ruler or template, cut 3 or 4 wedges 8½" long from this pieced block. You can vary the placement of the ruler to make wedges in different widths.

❹ Repeat Steps 1–3 to make 9 pieced wedges. *Fig. B*

MAKE A WEDGE SET THAT CHANGES DIRECTION

1 Join 5 or 6 wedges to make a rough square at least 8½″ in length.

2 Trim to 8½″ wide. *Fig. A*

3 Use the wedge ruler or template to add angles to the top and bottom of the square, as shown. *Fig. B*

4 Use this shape as you piece strips (below), as if it were just a large wedge.

NOTE *The linen slipped around a bit as I joined the wedges, so some of the seams are slightly curved or not at precise 9° angles. These small imperfections give the quilt an antique, improvisational look that I love.*

MAKE THE STRIPS

1 Join plain wedges, pieced wedges, and wedge sets into sections 12″–16″ long. Remember to alternate the wide end as you join wedges to keep the strip set straight. *Fig. C*

2 Arrange and join the sections to create 6 strips 66″ long. Press.

3 Join the strips together to complete the quilt top. Trim the edges even at the top and bottom.

FINISH THE QUILT

Layer the backing, batting, and quilt top. Baste and quilt by hand or machine. Then trim and bind!

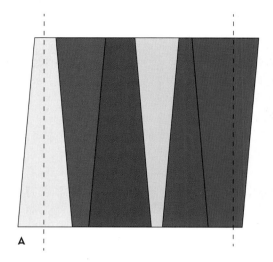

A

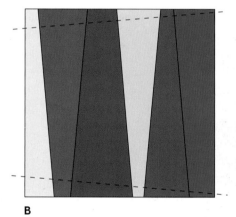

B

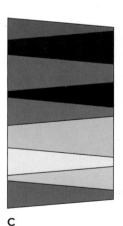

C

POP ART

88½″ × 88½″, designed and made
by Christina Cameli, quilted by Nancy Stovall

The real magic of what wedges can do is all here, where squared-off rounds come together in a psychedelic pattern that's not at all difficult to pull off.

Materials

Yardages are based on 40" usable width.

WHITE: 7 yards

ORANGE: 2¾ yards

PURPLE: 3¼ yards

RED: 3¼ yards

BACKING: 8⅛ yards, pieced to 97" × 97"

BATTING: 97" × 97"

BINDING: ⅔ yard

FREEZER PAPER

- -

Cutting

Make templates with the 6¾" set-in circle pattern and the Pop Art 9° wedge pattern (pullout page P2), or use a 9° wedge ruler.

WEDGES

Subcut wedges from the following strips. Rotate the template or ruler between cuts, as shown in Reciprocal Cutting (page 14). Take care to align the wide end of the template with the raw edge of the fabric.

From the white:

- Cut 18 strips 13½" × the width of fabric.

  Subcut 320 wedges.

From the orange:

- Cut 4 strips 13½" × the width of fabric.

  Subcut 64 wedges.

From the purple:

- Cut 8 strips 13½" × the width of fabric.

  Subcut 128 wedges.

From the red:

- Cut 8 strips 13½" × the width of fabric.

  Subcut 128 wedges.

CIRCLE CENTERS

From the orange:

- Cut 4 strips 8" × the width of fabric.

  Subcut 16 squares 8" × 8".

- -

Quilt Construction

Refer to Basic Round Construction (page 18) to learn how to construct the wedge sets. Use ¼" seams and press all seams open. Join wedges together from the wide end toward the narrow end.

MAKE THE WEDGE SETS

❶ Join the wedges into the following units. Make 64 of each. *Figs. A & B*

❷ Press. Trim the wedge sets using the 45° line on your cutting mat (page 21).

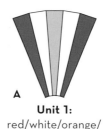

A

Unit 1:
red/white/orange/ white/red

B

Unit 2:
white/purple/white/ purple/white

MAKE THE ROUNDS

See Rounds That Behave (page 20) to learn how to check and trim your wedge sets at each step: 45°, 90°, and 180°.

❶ Form the quarter-rounds by joining a unit 1 and a unit 2 together. Keep the color placement the same in each quarter-round so they will be identical. *Fig. C*

❷ Trim the quarter-rounds using the perpendicular lines on your cutting mat (page 23).

❸ Form the half-rounds by joining 2 quarter-rounds.

❹ Form the full rounds by joining 2 half-rounds.

❺ Make 16 full rounds.

FINISH THE CENTERS

Use the set-in circle template to add an inner circle to each block (refer to Set-In Circles, page 97).

TRIM THE ROUNDS INTO SQUARES

❶ Fold each orange wedge in half, and finger-press to mark the center.

❷ Using a rotary cutting ruler, trim each round from these marked points to create 22½″ × 22½″ squares. *Figs. D & E*

ASSEMBLE THE QUILT TOP

❶ Sew the trimmed blocks into 4 rows of 4 blocks each, taking care to match the diagonal seams.

❷ Sew the rows together to complete the quilt top, taking care to match the seams.

FINISH THE QUILT

Layer the backing, batting, and quilt top. Baste and quilt by hand or machine. Then trim and bind!

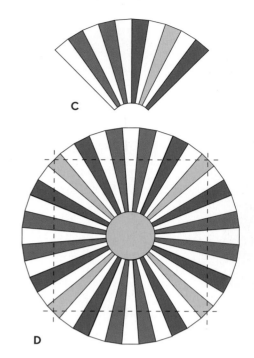

C

D

E

Quilt assembly

SEA OF SERENITY

55½″ × 57½″; designed, made, and quilted by Christina Cameli

An ocean of blues to wrap a little one in and to keep your world calm, no matter what storms may blow.

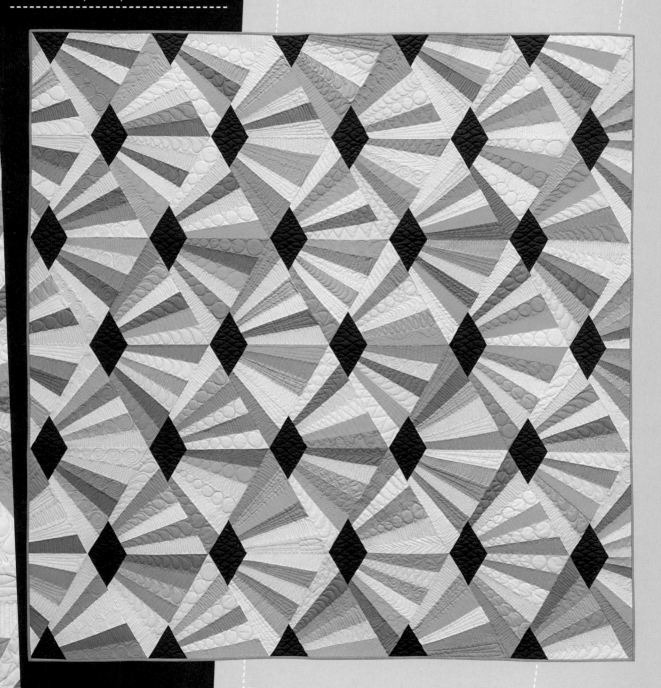

Materials

Yardages are based on 40" usable width, except where noted.

ASSORTED PRINTS OR SOLIDS: ⅝ yard *each* of 44"-wide fabric in 9 colors for wedges (⅞ yard if fabric is narrower)

DARK FABRIC: ⅞ yard for triangle points

BACKING: 3⅝ yards, pieced to 64" × 66"

BATTING: 64" × 66"

BINDING: ½ yard

CUTTING MAT WITH 60° GUIDE (*optional*)

Cutting

Make a template with the Sea of Serenity 10° wedge pattern (pullout page P2), or use a 10° wedge ruler. Make a template with the 60° corner trimming pattern (pullout page P2), or use a 60° corner trimmer.

ASSORTED PRINTS OR SOLIDS

From each color:

• Cut 2 strips 9" × the width of fabric.

Layer the strips and subcut wedges. Rotate the template or ruler between cuts, as shown in Reciprocal Cutting (page 14). Cut a total of 396 wedges. *Fig. A*

DARK FABRIC

• Cut 6 strips 4½" × the width of fabric.

Use the 60° line on your regular rotary ruler to cut 66 triangles, as shown. *Figs. B & C*

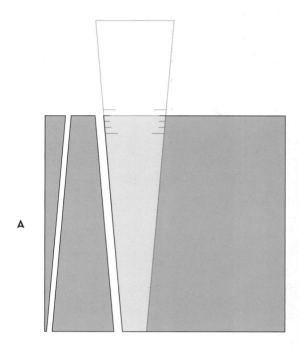

A

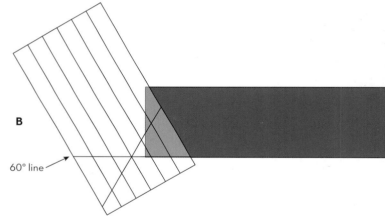

B

60° line

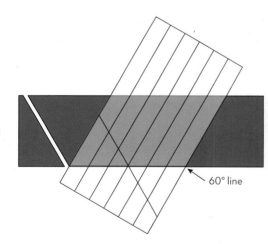

C

60° line

Quilt Construction

Refer to Basic Round Construction (page 18) to learn how to construct the wedge sets. Use ¼" seams and press all seams open. Join wedges together from the wide end toward the narrow end.

CREATE THE WEDGE SETS

❶ Join the wedges together randomly in sets of 2 to create 198 wedge pairs.

NOTE *The only rule I followed was not to sew two wedges of the same color together.*

❷ Join 3 wedge pairs to create a wedge set. You will have 66 wedge sets. Press.

❸ If you have a 60° mark on your cutting mat, trim the wedge sets to 60°. Refer to Trimming 10° Wedges (page 23). *Fig. D*

MAKE THE TRIANGLE BLOCKS

❶ Using a rotary cutter and straight ruler, cut each wedge set from corner to corner on the wide edge. Use the lines on the ruler to ensure that the cut is perpendicular to the center seam of the wedge set. *Fig. E*

❷ Trim the curved narrow end of the wedge sets 7¼" from the first cut. *Fig. F*

❸ Find the center of a triangle side and finger-press. Match this center point with the center seam of the narrow end of your trimmed wedge set. Join. Press. *Fig. G*

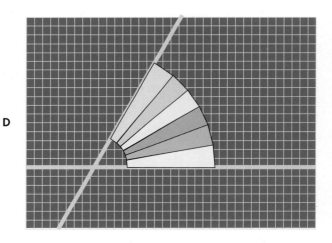

D

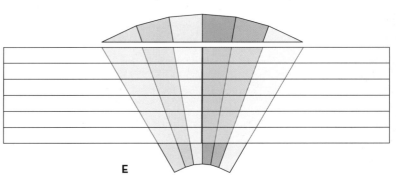

E

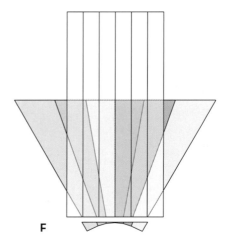

F

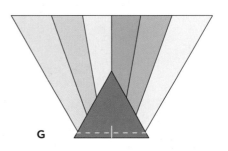

G

④ Trim the small triangles to size by aligning the quilting ruler with the edge of each wedge set and trimming the excess triangle fabric. Do this on both sides of the triangle. *Fig. H*

MAKE WEDGE DIAMONDS

❶ Set aside 10 pieced triangle blocks. Join the remaining triangle blocks in pairs so that the triangle tips meet along one edge, taking care to match the seams. You will have 28 block pairs.

❷ To help you align the pieces as you sew them together, use a 60° corner-trimming template to trim away the small point of the triangles. After you have trimmed the tips, you will be able to align the pieces perfectly for stitching. See Sewing Angled Pieces Accurately (page 100). *Fig. I*

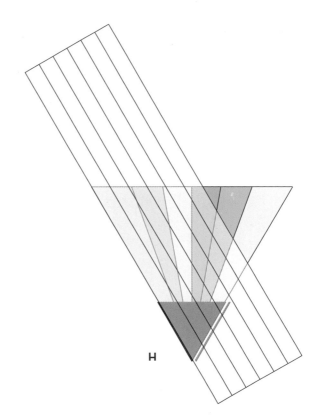

H

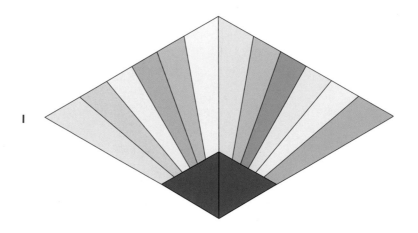

I

ASSEMBLE THE QUILT TOP

❶ Arrange the wedge diamonds and triangle blocks diagonally. *Fig. J*

❷ Join the diamonds and triangles into diagonal rows, as shown. Press.

❸ Join the rows, taking care to match the points. Press.

❹ Trim the right and left sides of the quilt in straight lines by making vertical cuts ¼" from the points.

FINISH THE QUILT

Layer the backing, batting, and quilt top. Baste and quilt by hand or machine. Then trim and bind!

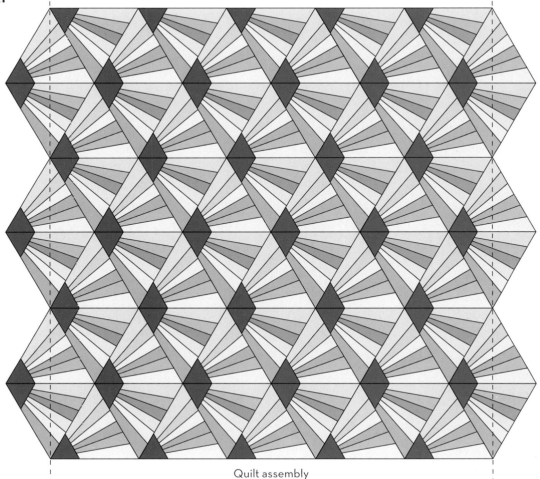

J

Quilt assembly

PRISMATIC

58" × 68½", designed and made
by Christina Cameli, quilted by Nancy Stovall

If you have a lot of fabric in your stash, here is a quilt to bring vibrancy and sparkle into your world. It's surprisingly straightforward to make!

Materials

Yardages are based on 40" usable width.

ASSORTED SOLIDS: 7" × 33" rectangles in 36 colors for wedges (Choose 6 color groups of 6 fabrics each.)

ADDITIONAL ASSORTED SOLIDS: 6 scraps at least 5" × 5" for center (Choose each scrap from a different color group so that all 6 groups are represented.)

BLACK: 1½ yards

BACKING: 3¾ yards, pieced to 66" × 77"

BATTING: 66" × 77"

BINDING: ½ yard

Cutting

Make a template with the Prismatic *10° wedge pattern (pullout page P2), or use a 10° wedge ruler and extension for making 70" circles. Make a template with the 60° corner trimming pattern (pullout page P2), or use a 60° corner trimmer.*

ASSORTED SOLIDS

From each color:

• Cut 1 wedge using the wedge template or ruler. If you are using an acrylic ruler with an extension, hold the 2 rulers together with packing tape for stability while cutting. See Keeping Your Ruler Steady (page 15).

ADDITIONAL ASSORTED SOLIDS

• Trim each scrap to 5" × 5" square.

BLACK

• Cut 9 strips 1" × the width of fabric for the accent strips.

From 3 strips, subcut 6 rectangles 1" × 16".

From each of the remaining strips, subcut 1 rectangle 1" × 26" and 1 rectangle 1" × 5".

• Cut 2 rectangles 18⅜" × 31¼" for the corner triangles.

Subcut the rectangles in half diagonally. To make this easier, try aligning the short edges of 2 long quilting rulers to create a long straight edge that will reach from corner to corner. Use packing tape to hold the 2 rulers together temporarily. *Fig. A*

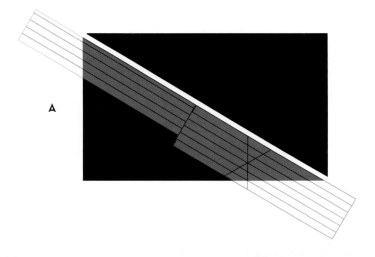

A

Quilt Construction

Refer to Basic Round Construction (page 18) to learn how to construct the wedge sets. Use ¼″ seams and press all seams open. Join wedges together from the wide end toward the narrow end.

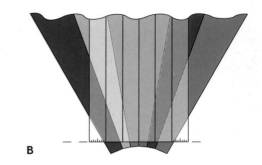

B

CREATE THE WEDGE SETS

❶ Join the wedges into sets of 6 wedges each, grouped by color. Take care to align the top edges and pin the seams to avoid stretching pieces while sewing the long seams. Press.

❷ Trim the bottom edges of each wedge set at the point where the unit is 4¼″ across. Use the vertical lines on your quilting ruler to make sure your cut is perpendicular to the center seam of the wedge set. *Fig. B*

❸ Use a quilting ruler to make a cut 9″ above the first cut. Again, use the lines on the quilting ruler to make sure this cut is perpendicular to the center seam of the wedge set. To check your measurement before you cut, the length of the angled edge of the cut wedge section should be about 10½″. *Fig. C*

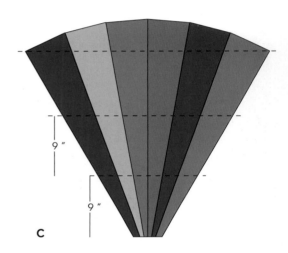

9 ″

9 ″

C

❹ Repeat Step 3 to make another cut 9″ from the newly cut edge.

❺ For the remaining wedge section, trim the end straight by cutting from corner to corner using 2 rulers taped together.

D

JOINING THE ACCENT STRIPS

❶ Join a 16″ black accent strip to the narrow end of each middle wedge section. To align the strip correctly, find the midpoint of the strip and align it with the center seam of the wedge section. Press. Do not trim the accent strip yet. *Fig. D*

❷ Use the same technique to join a 26″ black accent strip to the narrow end of each large wedge section. *Fig. E*

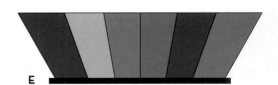

E

RECONSTRUCT THE WEDGE SECTIONS

❶ Rearrange the cut wedge sections so that the wedges are composed this way from the largest wedge section to the smallest:

Wedge 1: red, orange, yellow	**Wedge 4:** green, blue, purple
Wedge 2: orange, yellow, green	**Wedge 5:** blue, purple, red
Wedge 3: yellow, green, blue	**Wedge 6:** purple, red, orange

❷ Join the wedge sections, taking care to align the midpoints of the wedge sections as you join them. Trim the black accent strips even with the edges. Press.

ADD THE POINTS

❶ Sew a 5″ black accent strip to one side of each 5″ × 5″ center fabric.

❷ Coordinating the colors as listed at the right, join a unit from Step 1 to each wedge section. Take care to align the center of the black accent strip with the wedge section's center seam.

Wedge 1: green	**Wedge 4:** red
Wedge 2: blue	**Wedge 5:** orange
Wedge 3: purple	**Wedge 6:** yellow

❸ Trim the triangle point by aligning a quilting ruler with the edges of the wedge section and trimming the excess fabric. For increased precision, you can use a 60° triangle template. *Fig. F*

❹ To help you align the pieces as you sew them together, use a 60° corner-trimming template to trim away the small point of the triangles. After you have trimmed the tips, you will be able to align the pieces perfectly for stitching. See Sewing Angled Pieces Accurately (page 100).

ASSEMBLE THE QUILT TOP

❶ Arrange the wedge triangles in a hexagon, in order from 1 to 6.

❷ Join 3 wedges together to make a half-hexagon, taking care to match the black strips. Press. *Fig. G*

❸ Join the half-hexagons together, again taking care to match the black strips. Press.

❹ Orient the hexagon so that the right and left sides are vertical and there is a right and left corner at the top and bottom.

❺ Join a large black triangle to each corner of the quilt. See Sewing Angled Pieces Accurately (page 100). Press.

FINISH THE QUILT

Layer the backing, batting, and quilt top. Baste and quilt by hand or machine. Then trim and bind!

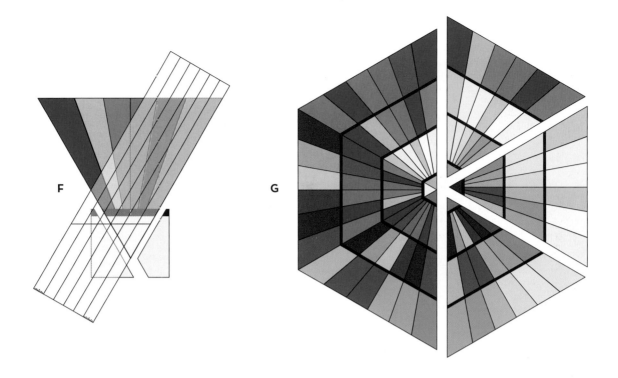

F

G

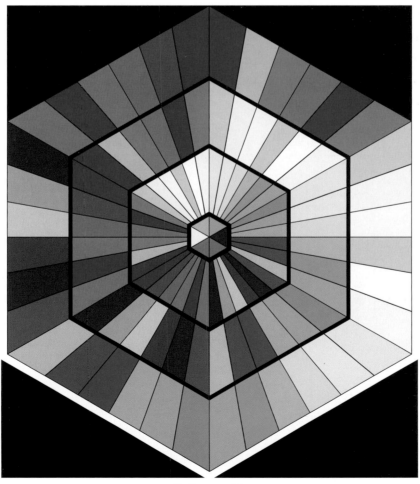

Quilt assembly

DIAMOND CHAIN

80½" × 91½", designed and
made by Christina Cameli, quilted
by Christina Cameli and Nancy Stovall

*Diamonds? You're worth it! Drape
yourself in jewels, and go all out
with chartreuse and blues!*

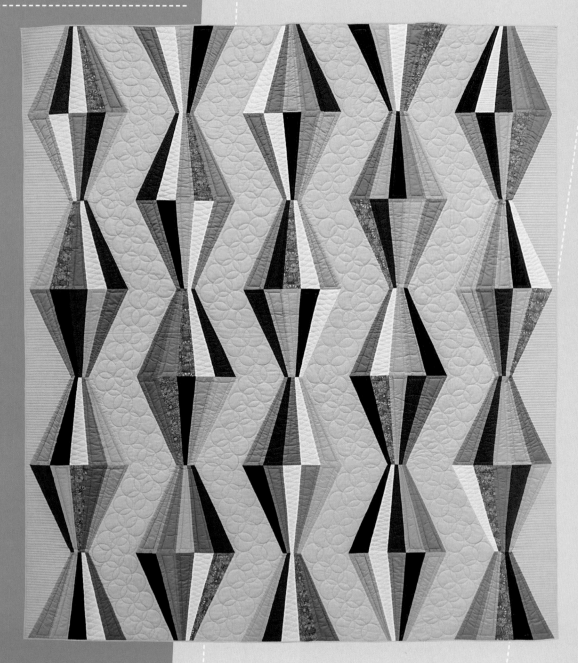

Materials

Yardages are based on 40" usable width, except where noted.

ASSORTED SOLIDS: 1 yard *each* of 7 different solid colors

ACCENT PRINT: 1/2 yard of 44"-wide fabric

BACKGROUND SOLID: 3¾ yards

BACKING: 7½ yards, pieced to 89" × 100"

BATTING: 89" × 100"

BINDING: ⅔ yard

NOTE *If your 1/2 yard of accent print has 44" usable width, you will be able to cut 16 accent wedges, which is the number of print wedges I used in my quilt. If your fabric is narrower, you may be able to cut only 15 print wedges from 1/2 yard. But you will have plenty of solid fabric for an extra wedge, so you can replace that last print wedge with a solid one.*

Cutting

Make a template with the Diamond Chain *10° wedge pattern (pullout page P2), or use a 10° wedge ruler.*

Subcut wedges from the following strips. Rotate the template or ruler between cuts, as shown in Reciprocal Cutting (page 14). Take care to align the wide end of the template with the raw edge of the fabric. To save time, you can carefully layer two strips before you subcut the wedges.

ASSORTED SOLIDS

From each color:

• Cut 2 strips 16" × the width of fabric.

  Subcut 24 wedges, 168 total in all colors.

ACCENT PRINT

• Cut a strip 16" × the width of fabric.

  Subcut 16 wedges.

BACKGROUND SOLID

• Cut 9 strips 14" × the width of fabric.

  Subcut 35 rectangles 8⅝" × 14". You should get 4 rectangles per strip.

  Subcut each rectangle in half diagonally using the following method: Orient the rectangle on your cutting mat vertically, with the long ends at the sides. Place a mark on the top edge 1" from the top right corner and on the bottom edge 1" from the bottom left corner. Align your ruler between these 2 points, and cut the rectangle diagonally. *Fig. A*

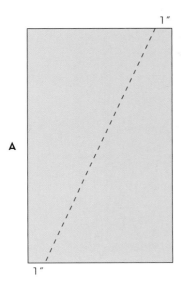

Quilt Construction

Refer to Basic Round Construction (page 18) to learn how to construct the wedge sets. Use ¼″ seams and press all seams open. Join wedges together from the wide end toward the narrow end.

CREATE THE WEDGE SETS

❶ Join the wedges randomly into sets of 5 wedges each. Make a total of 35 wedge sets. Press.

❷ Find the midpoint of the middle wedge in each wedge set by folding it in half lengthwise. Finger-press at both the wide end and narrow end.

❸ Using a quilting ruler, make a horizontal cut even with the narrow end of the middle wedge. Use the markings on your quilting ruler to ensure that the cut remains perpendicular to the finger-pressed centerline. *Fig. B*

❹ Cut the wide edge straight by measuring 14″ from the first cut and cutting again, using the markings on your quilting ruler to ensure that the cut remains perpendicular to the finger-pressed centerline. *Fig. C*

CREATE THE BLOCKS

Attach a background half-rectangle to each side of a trimmed wedge set. Press. Be sure to align the pieces so that the seam begins in the correct location ¼″ from the edge (see Sewing Angled Pieces Accurately, page 100). Repeat for all 35 wedge sets. *Fig. D*

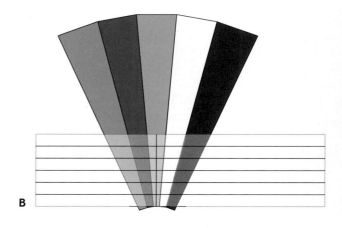

B

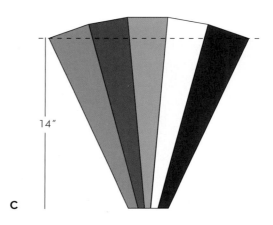

14″

C

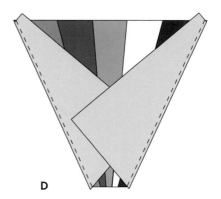

D

ASSEMBLE THE QUILT TOP

❶ Set aside 5 blocks.

❷ Join the remaining blocks in pairs at the wide wedge end, taking care to match the seams.

❸ Join the block pairs into columns of 3 block pairs each.

❹ Add one of the reserved single blocks to the end of each column. Press

❺ Arrange the columns in alternate directions as shown, and join to complete the quilt top. Press.

FINISH THE QUILT

Layer the backing, batting, and quilt top. Baste and quilt by hand or machine. Then trim and bind!

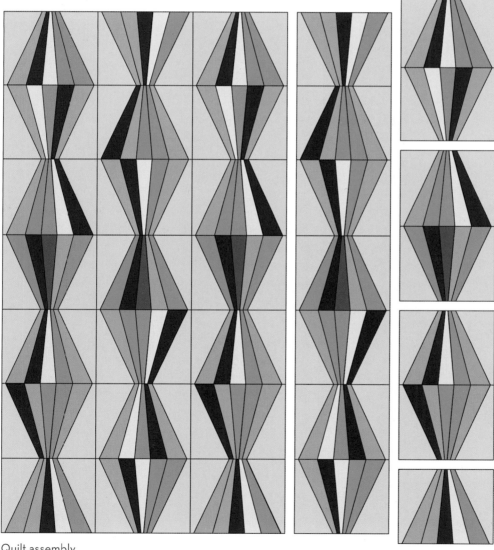

Quilt assembly

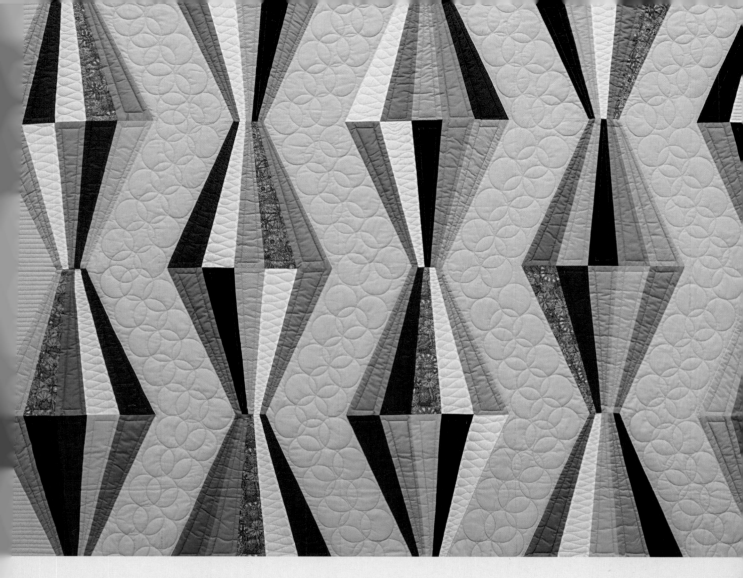

Something Else to Try

Changing the orientation of the pieced sections allows you to make serpentine paths instead of rounds with your wedge units. There are so many possibilities!

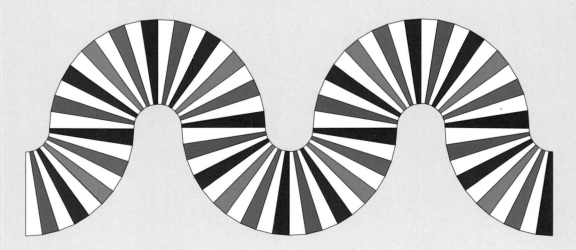

SKILLS AND TECHNIQUES

Machine Appliqué

For finishing the raw edge of a round, particularly the outer edge of a full-size round, the quickest approach is machine appliqué. This method is used on the outer edges of the *Good Night, Good Morning* round (page 44) and both edges of *Half and Half* (page 32). The zigzag or straight stitch can be used for machine appliqué.

❶ To prepare a round for machine appliqué, place it right side down on your ironing surface, and press the raw edge to the back ¼".

❷ Lay out the background on which the round is to be appliquéd. If you need to, press a center-line into the background, and use this to align the seams or centers of the wedges.

❸ Place the round right side up on the background, taking care to orient the round correctly if it has a top side. Smooth the round so that it is

flat and not distorted. Pin in place, or tack with temporary sewing glue.

❹ Using a topstitch needle, topstitch the round to the background right along the edge of the round. Use a straight or zigzag stitch (I recommend a stitch length of 2.0 and a stitch width of 3.0 for zigzag). Your machine may have other specialty stitches you can use for appliqué. Be sure to back-stitch when you start and stop, or pull your top thread to the back to knot with the bobbin thread.

96   WEDGE QUILT WORKSHOP

Hand Appliqué

Hand appliqué is ideal for attaching a round to a background without having visible stitches. It takes longer, but that can be one of its benefits: a little time to slow down and sew!

❶ Use a hand-sewing needle and fine thread that matches the appliqué fabric color. Knot the thread.

❷ Bring the needle up from behind the background fabric, as close as possible to the edge of the appliqué fabric.

❸ Catch a few threads of the folded appliqué edge; then put the needle back down into the background fabric near the stitch you just took.

❹ Travel underneath the background fabric, and bring the needle back up about 1/8″ away.

❺ Repeat Steps 3 and 4 all the way around the folded edge of the appliqué. When you finish, bring the needle to the back of the background and knot it off.

Set-In Circles

Finishing the open center of a round can be done by hand or machine appliqué, but there is a simple way to piece the circle using a piece of freezer paper to help create a stitching guide. I used this technique in *The Three of Us* (page 58) and *Pop Art* (page 74).

Supplies

FREEZER PAPER: 12″ × 12″ square

TEMPLATE FOR THE DESIRED FINISHED-SIZE CIRCLE (For most of the quilts in this book, make a template from the 6¾″ set-in circle pattern, pullout page P2.)

PENCIL

SCISSORS for cutting paper

COMPLETED WEDGE ROUND

TEMPORARY (WASHABLE) FABRIC GLUE

FABRIC FOR THE FINISHED CIRCLE: About 1″ bigger in diameter than the finished dimensions of the circle

SEWING MACHINE WITH A ZIPPER FOOT

SEW THE SET-IN CIRCLE

❶ Carefully center the circle template onto the dull side of the freezer paper square. Trace around the template.

❷ Using sharp scissors, carefully cut the circle out from the center, leaving the edges of the freezer paper intact. *Fig. A*

❸ Lay the round to be finished right side down on your ironing surface, making sure that it is flat and not distorted. Position the freezer paper with the shiny side down, aligned over the hole.

❹ With the iron on a warm setting, press the freezer paper to the back of the pieced round. The warmth will cause the freezer paper to adhere until you pull it off.

❺ Increase the iron heat to high, and press the seam allowance of the inner circle to the back along the edge of the freezer-paper template. *Fig. B*

❻ Apply a scant amount of temporary glue to the top of the pressed-back seam allowance. *Fig. C*

❼ While the glue is wet, lay the center circle fabric facedown over the hole. Smooth it with your hand from the center outward, pressing the fabric over the glued seam allowance. Be sure the seam allowance is glued around the entire circle. *Fig. D*

❽ Allow the glue to dry, pressing to speed up this process if necessary.

❾ Remove the freezer-paper template by peeling from a corner. Set it aside to be reused; it will stick for several uses.

❿ Install a zipper foot on your sewing machine. Use a straight-stitch setting.

⓫ With the center circle fabric on the bottom, begin stitching in the folded line created by ironing back the seam allowance of the round. Stitch around the entire circle, moving the round fabric out of the way as you go. Be careful to keep the center circle fabric from folding under itself as you go. *Fig. E*

⓬ Check that your circle looks right from the front. Trim away the excess seam allowance from the square of center circle fabric. Press the seam allowances toward or away from the center as desired.

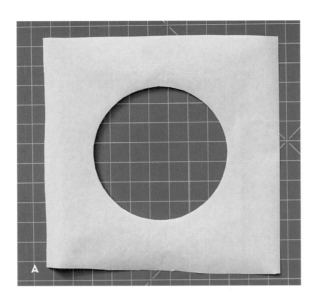

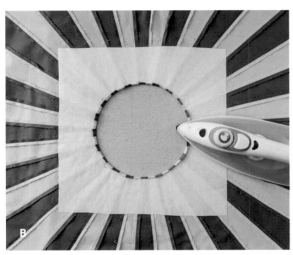

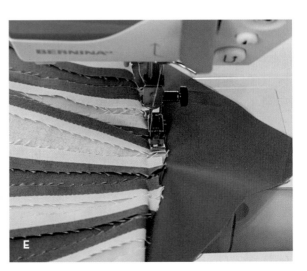

Sewing Angled Pieces Accurately

When sewing angled pieces together to create a row, as in *It Takes All Sorts* (page 68); to attach background pieces, as in *Diamond Chain* (page 90); or to join diamond shapes, as in *Sea of Serenity* (page 78); the pieces need to be aligned so that when the seam is sewn ¼″ from the raw edge, the piece opens to create a continuous edge. If the pieces are not aligned correctly before you stitch, they will be offset when opened, and you will have an uneven edge on which to join the next pieces.

These two pieces were aligned with the raw edges matching, which makes for uneven edges once the seam is pressed open.

These two pieces were aligned so that the line of stitching falls in the correct place and creates an even edge when the seam is pressed open.

There are tools available to make aligning some angled shapes easier. For the angles in this book that are 60°, such as *Sea of Serenity* (page 78), you can use a corner-trimming tool for 60° angles. Before you begin piecing your angled pieces, place the trimming tool on the shape and trim away the small point of the triangle. Then use the trimmed point to align the shapes you are joining. If you do not have a trimming tool, you can make a template from the 60° corner trimming pattern (pullout page P2).

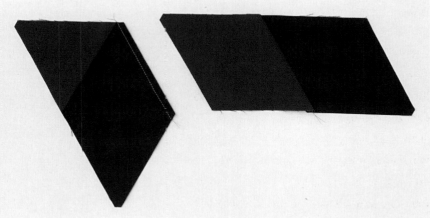

If you are working with nonstandard angles, as with some of the quilts in this book, you can easily align your pieces using your quilting ruler and a temporary marking pencil or pen. On the back of the piece that will be on top when you sew, place a mark ¼" from the edge on either end. These marks show where the stitching line will start and stop. When aligning the marked piece with the piece you will be joining, make sure the mark falls at the point where the raw edges intersect. Pin in place and sew with a ¼" seam. With practice, some quilters can estimate this distance without marking.

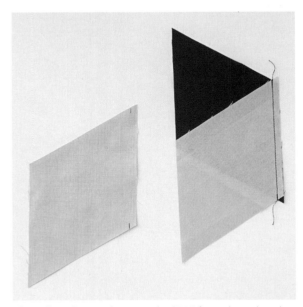

The yellow diamond was marked ¼" from the right edge, and the marked lines were then aligned with the raw edges of the red diamond. Note how the ¼" seam falls in the "valley" created by the two raw edges.

Quilting Suggestions

Many quilting designs fit well into wedge shapes. Here are some examples to consider.

HOW TO AVOID RIPPLING

If your quilting is very dense where the wedges come into the center but less dense in the center itself or on the outer part of the wedges, it may distort the quilt, and you may have difficulty keeping the center flat. This is most likely to happen if you have multiple quilting lines converging in the center of a wedge round.

To avoid multiple lines converging in the center, you could have some of your quilting lines come to a point before reaching the center, as shown. Or you could begin with a less dense design, like a single line, and begin adding density once you are in a larger area of the wedge.

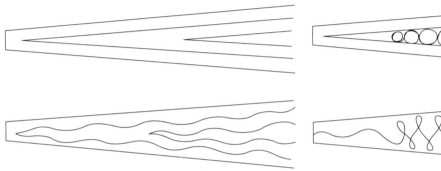
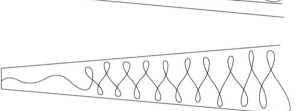

BLOCKING A QUILT

If your quilt won't lie flat after it has been quilted, you can fix the problem by blocking your quilt. You can block the quilt before or after you have attached the binding.

❶ To block a quilt, lay it out faceup and flat on the floor. If you have a carpeted floor, pin the quilt to the carpet with sturdy pins. If you have a wood floor, tape the edge of the quilt top so that it is taut and any ripples are flattened. (Alternatively, you could use foam core boards underneath the quilt to give you something to pin the quilt in place against.)

❷ Measure the edges of the quilt top to make sure the quilt is the same width along the top and bottom, and the same length along the right and left sides. Adjust your pins or tape if necessary.

❸ Using a spray bottle filled with water, thoroughly spritz the entire quilt top so that it is heavy and wet. Pat down any areas that bubble up until they lie flat. Now let the quilt air-dry. (Running a fan in the room while blocking can speed this process along.) Blocking can eliminate contortions of the quilt top quite well.

AFTERWORD:
THE MAKING OF *SACRED HEART*

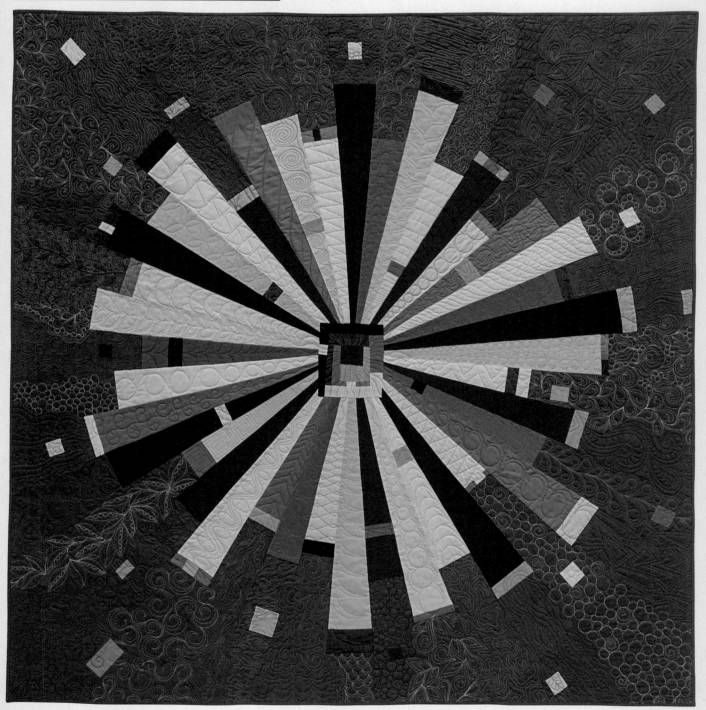

Sacred Heart, 57½″ × 59″

My goal in writing this book was to show you everything I've learned so far about wedges so you could recreate some of my quilts or design your own. To end the book, I'd like to take you through the creative process of making *Sacred Heart*, a quilt I showed you way back in the introduction.

Sacred Heart was made using a 9° ruler, but it was done in a less systematic manner than the other quilts in this book. I have a penchant for improvisation and a willingness to design as I go. This means that I did things as the quilt developed that I would have approached differently if I had started with a clear plan for the quilt. I didn't have a plan though, and maybe that's how you work sometimes, too. So here's how I made this quilt work.

As I began working on *Sacred Heart*, I had only a general idea of what it would look like. I knew that I wanted the square block in the middle and wedges of different lengths exploding out from the center. I cut wedges of different lengths and set them up on my design wall.

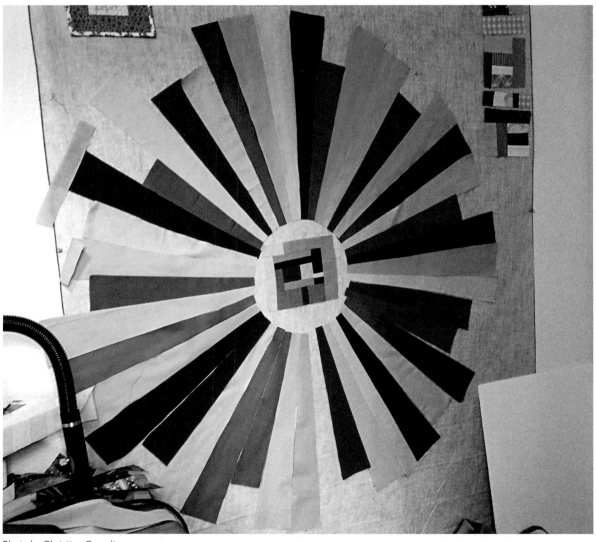

Photo by Christina Cameli

I discovered that I wanted the wedges to have interruptions occasionally, so I sliced them crosswise, inserted a scrap, and then recut the wedge shape. This was an imprecise process that resulted in some wedges shrinking in length. Given the improvisational nature of the design, however, this wasn't a problem for me.

To make all the wedges a consistent length, I added background fabric to the end of each wedge. I also inserted little scraps into some of the background fabrics. Afterward, I recut the piece to a wedge shape using the wedge ruler. The size wedge I wanted was longer than my ruler, so I used my quilting ruler to extend the angle of the edges.

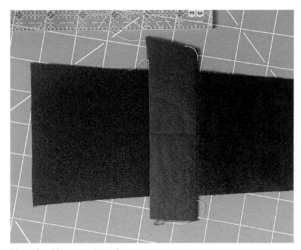

Photo by Christina Cameli

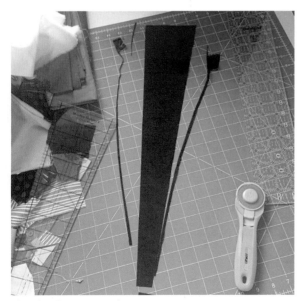

Photo by Christina Cameli

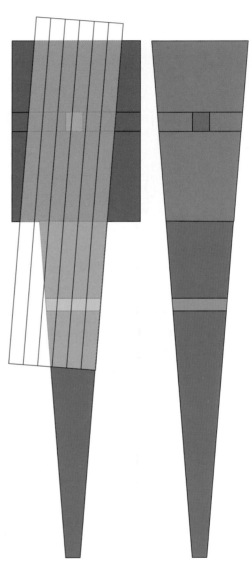

I sewed the wedges together in groups of five for eighth-rounds. I trimmed these using the 45° angle on my cutting mat (page 21). Then I cut those five-wedge sections in a straight line from corner to corner; this created an octagon shape when all eight sections were joined. This is how *The Three of Us* (page 58) was made.

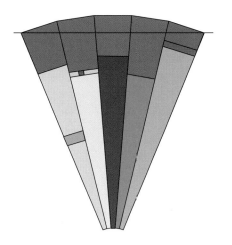

Photo by Christina Cameli

To finish the square quilt top, I estimated the size of the triangle needed to complete the corner of the octagon. I pieced the triangles of background fabric with little bright scraps inserted, constructing them slightly larger than I needed. I attached these triangles to the corners of the octagon and trimmed away the excess triangle fabric. Then I stitched the Log Cabin block over the center opening of the round.

Photo by Christina Cameli

When I quilted *Sacred Heart*, I was thinking a lot about my grandmother's influence on my creative journey; I wanted the quilting to reflect that. Every wedge was quilted individually. A wavy line radiates from the center square and becomes a geometric pattern in the wedges. At the end of the wedge, it changes to a more organic pattern and swirls and bumps against nearby designs. The pattern moves from order into chaos and is also a way for me to show how one woman's spirit reverberates through time and space in a beautiful, uncontrollable tapestry that carries on and on.

If you were creating a quilt like this, you could certainly improv your way through it as I did.

However, if you want to cut each wedge easily and only once, I would advise the following:

• Piecing the entire unit first and then cutting the wedge shape

• Using a wedge ruler and wedge extension ruler if you need a larger wedge than what your ruler provides

However you go about creating your wedge quilt, the same concepts apply. Whether you plan everything in advance or like to play along the way, your style can shine through with wedges.

If you make something you're proud of, I'd love to hear from you! Send me a picture at afewscraps@gmail.com.

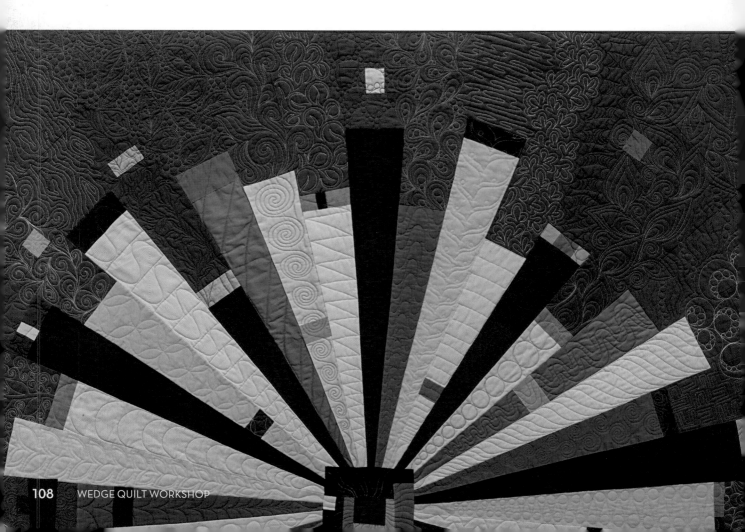

DESIGN SHEETS

Feel free to copy and use these drawings to plan your own wedge quilt.

9° Round

A 50″ circle with a 6″ center. This circle requires
40 wedges cut from a 9° wedge template.

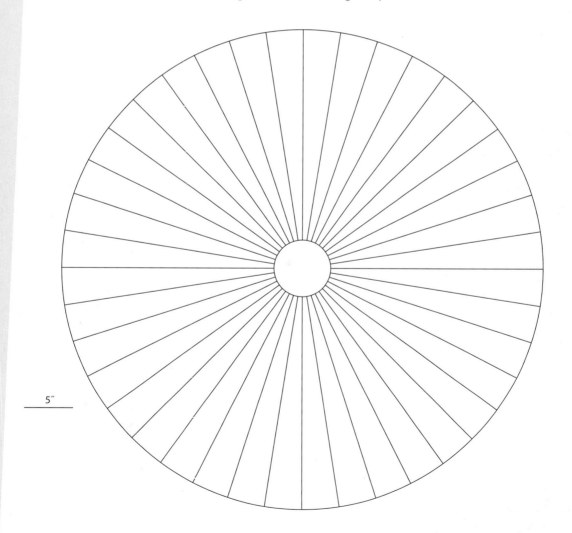

5″

10° Round

A 50" circle with a 6" center. This circle requires
36 wedges cut from a 10° wedge template.

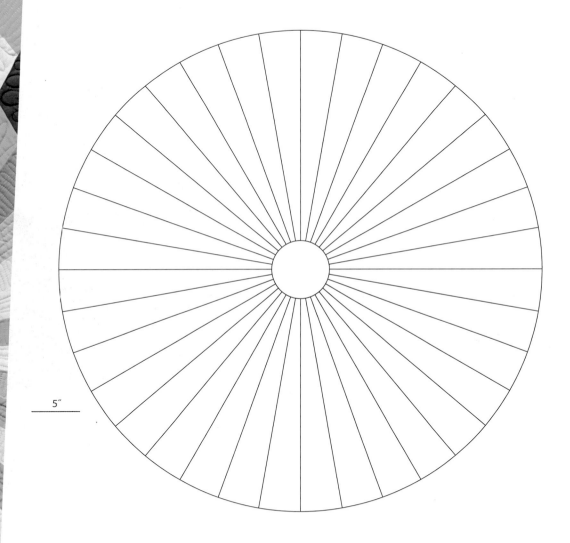

5″

ABOUT THE AUTHOR

Christina Cameli *is an enthusiastic quilting teacher and nurse-midwife living with her children in Portland, Oregon. After being introduced to quilting by her grandmother, she learned free-motion quilting and over the next decade began teaching classes. She is the author of* First Steps to Free-Motion Quilting *and* Step-by-Step Free-Motion Quilting *(both by C&T Publishing). She loves spreading the joy of quilting far and wide by teaching around the country and online.*

Follow Christina on social media:

Website: www.afewscraps.com
Instagram: @afewscraps

Christina Cameli

Resources

9° Wedge Ruler
dohenypublications.com

10° Wedge Ruler
phillipsfiberart.com
creativegridsusa.com

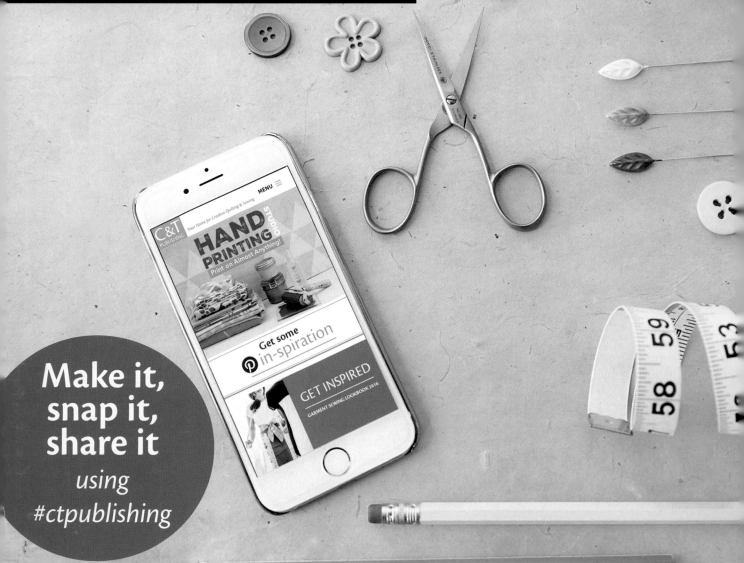